**FRIENDS
OF ACPL**

W9-AXI-094

**DO NOT REMOVE
CARDS FROM POCKET**

Ghana
Mali
Songhay

FRONT COVER: This artifact from Mali is made of wood, iron, and fibre, and represents the head and antlers of an antelope.

African Kingdoms of the Past

Ghana
Mali
Songhay

·

The
Western
Sudan

Kenny Mann

Dillon Press • Parsippany, New Jersey

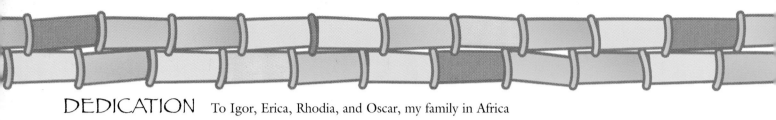

DEDICATION
To Igor, Erica, Rhodia, and Oscar, my family in Africa

ACKNOWLEDGMENTS
The author wishes to acknowledge the interest, patience, and expertise of the following consultants: Clarence G. Seckel, Jr., Curriculum Coordinator of Social Studies, School District 189, East St. Louis, IL; and Edna J. Whitfield, Social Studies Supervisor (retired), St. Louis Public Schools, MI.

CREDITS
Design and Illustration: MaryAnn Zanconato
Picture Research: Kenny Mann

PHOTO CREDITS
Abbas/Magnum: 52–53, 55, 57; American Museum of Natural History: 38–39; Angela Fisher & Carol Beckwith/Robert Estall: 20; Bruce Coleman Inc./S.C. Carton: D; Carol Beckwith/Robert Estall: 15, 35, 41, 95; Collection of American Numismatic Society: 24; George Gerster/Comstock: 17; Hoa-Qui/Liaison International: 44; James Stanfield/National Geographic Society: 18–19; New York Public Library: 70; New York Public Library, Schomburg Center: 63; Photograph by Eliot Elisofon, National Museum of African Art, Eliot Elisofon Photographic Archives, Smithsonian Institution: 65, 78–79, 92–93; Photograph by Franko Khoury, National Museum of African Art, Eliot Elisofon Photographic Archives, Smithsonian Institution: Cover, 61; Photograph by J.B.Thorpe, American Museum of Natural History: 78; Rod McIntosh: 13, 27; SBG, Courtesy American Museum of Natural History: 73; 84; SBG Steve McCurry/Magnum: 38. Maps, Ortelius Design: 4, 36–37, 75.

Library of Congress Cataloging-in-Publication Data
Mann, Kenny.
    Ghana, Mali, Songhay: the Western Sudan/ by Kenny Mann. — 1st ed.
    p. cm. — (African kingdoms of the past)
    Includes bibliographical references and index.
    ISBN 0-87518-656-4 — ISBN 0-382-39176-4 (pbk.)
    1. Ghana Empire—History. 2. Songhay Empire —History 3. Mali Empire — History. I. Title. II. Series.
DT532.15.M36   1996
966.1'016—dc20   95-16061
Summary: A study of the legends and history of the ancient West African kingdoms of Ghana, Mali, and Songhay, including background and commentary on Islam's influence in the region.

Published by Dillon Press,
A Division of Simon & Schuster,
299 Jefferson Road, Parsippany, NJ 07054

First edition
Printed in the United States of America
10 9 8 7 6 5 4 3 2 1

Table of Contents

Introduction

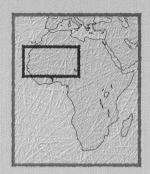

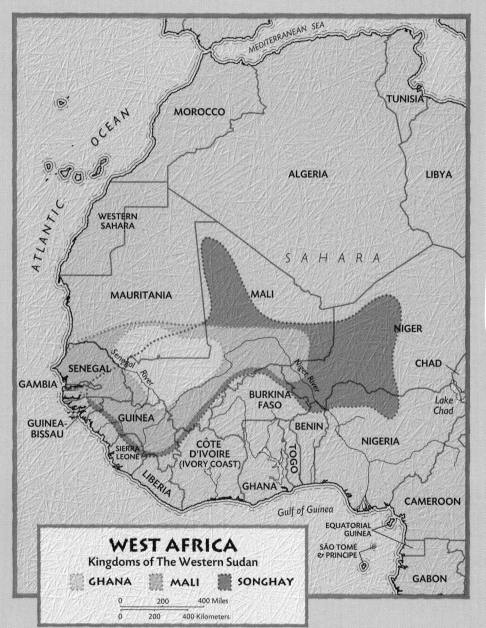

WEST AFRICA
Kingdoms of The Western Sudan

GHANA   MALI   SONGHAY

0   200   400 Miles
0   200   400 Kilometers

Southern Mauritania, Senegal, Mali, Burkina Faso, Niger, Northern Nigeria, and Chad—these are the modern nations that comprise the western Sudan.

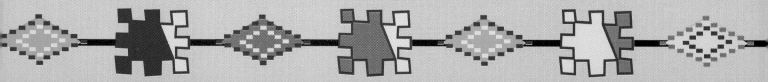

It is hard to imagine that the impoverished, drought-ridden area known today as the western Sudan was once a region where rich and powerful kingdoms flourished. What remains of the palaces so richly described by Arab travelers? Where are the battlegrounds where warriors fought as first one kingdom, then another rose to power? And where are the legendary mines that had for so long supplied Europeans with gold for their coins?

For centuries, Europeans heard only vague rumors about Ghana, the "land of gold." Arab travelers told tales of "the richest king in the world," thriving market cities, and huge armies of well-equipped soldiers. Exactly where Ghana was, however, they could not say. At that time there were no maps of Africa south of the Sahara. It was *terra incognita*, or "unknown land," and would remain so for many centuries to come.

The Arabs who supplied the first written accounts of the western Sudan followed merchants who crossed the Sahara along ancient trade routes. The first Europeans to arrive in West Africa came by sea. First the Portuguese, then other Europeans— all lured by tales of gold—arrived in the Gulf of Guinea (GIHN ee).* They came to trade, not to conquer.

The African leaders allowed the Europeans to establish trading posts on the Guinea coast. But the Africans had no intention of revealing the whereabouts of their gold mines and carefully restricted the Europeans' movements. Faced with large African armies and the unknown terrors of the interior, the Europeans willingly complied with the limitations placed on them. After all, African traders coming from far inland brought them all the gold, ivory, and slaves that they could want.

*Words that may be difficult to pronounce have been spelled phonetically in parentheses. A pronunciation key appears on page 97.

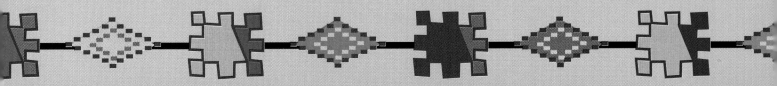

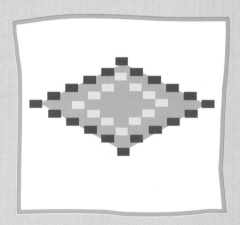

Thus there was little incentive for the Europeans to explore the western Sudan. It was not until the late eighteenth century, after 300 years of the slave trade, that European interest in Africa exploded. Politicians and businessmen dreamed of land and mineral resources that they could exploit. Adventurous farmers and settlers wanted new lands to colonize. And zealous missionaries looked forward to converting untold numbers of "savages" to Christianity.

In 1788, a group of British scholars formed the African Association to promote exploration. Seven years later the Scottish explorer Mungo Park traced the source of the Niger River. He found that it flowed east, not west, as had been reported. Between 1822 and 1824, Hugh Clapperton traveled south from Tripoli, in Libya, across the Sahara to Lake Chad, where the great kingdom of Kanem-Bornu still thrived. In 1826 the English explorer Gordon Laing became the first European to reach the city of Timbuktu, on the great bend of the Niger River. Soon afterward the French explorer René Caillié traveled along the Niger to Timbuktu and then north across the Sahara.

The western Sudan was now mapped and charted. But the European explorers had come too late to witness the splendor of the kingdoms of Ghana, and of Mali (MAH lee)and Songhay (SON gye), which rose to power after Ghana was defeated. These kingdoms had long since been

The Niger was so named by the Romans, who called it the "river of the black people." In Latin, the word *niger* (nih GAIR) means "black." In Spanish, the word for "black" is *negro* (NAY groh).

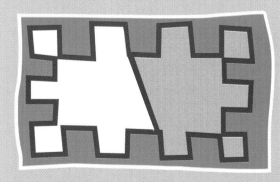

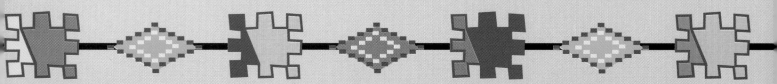

destroyed by internal power struggles and Islamic conquerors. From the fifteenth century on, they also suffered from European intervention in trade.

The histories of these kingdoms are told and retold in the oral tradition of

West Africa. A few written accounts by early Arab travelers also preserve details about the kingdoms. On the whole, however, European and African historians, archaeologists, and anthropologists have had to piece together the histories of the kingdoms bit by bit. Here, then, are the legends and histories of the kingdoms of Ghana, Mali, and Songhay, as we know them today. They are part of a heritage of which the people of the western Sudan are justly proud.

Europeans believed that before they arrived on the "dark continent," the Africans had no history. In the eyes of the Europeans, the Africans were "primitive children who had never grown up." It was not until the twentieth century that African and European leaders and historians succeeded in securing a place for African history in the scope of world events and in making the world powers aware of Africa's extraordinary achievements.

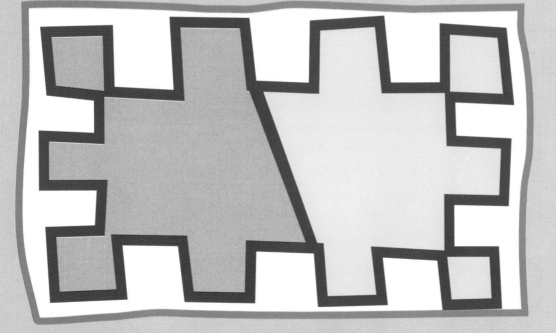

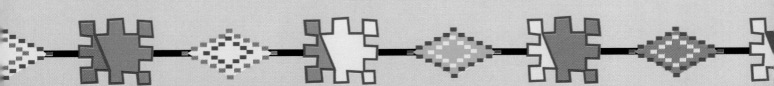

African Kingdoms

Note: Dates marked with an * are approximate.

4000	B.C.	A.D.	500	800	1100

*4000 B.C.	Sahara begins to dry out
*3200 B.C.	Earliest known writing in Mesopotamia; Menes becomes the first Pharaoh of Egypt
*2000 B.C.	Minoans establish civilization on Crete
*600 B.C.	Sahara becomes a desert
*500 B.C.	Persian empire at its height
*350 B.C.	Origins of earliest known Iron Age culture south of Sahara
525 B.C.	Start of Buddhism in northern India

A.D. 300–900	Mayan empire flourishes in Central America
570	Prophet Mohammed is born
622	Mohammed's flight from Mecca marks the Hegira
630	Mohammed returns to Mecca and destroys idols in the Kaaba
632	Mohammed dies
*700	Soninke people unite; Kumbi founded
*800	Ghana is established trading state; Charlemagne crowned Emperor of the Holy Roman Empire
970	First written records of Ghana compiled by Ibn Haukal

1003	Vikings reach Vinland (Newfoundland, Canada)
1009	Songhay king accepts Islam
1067	El-Bekri writes Book of Roads and Kingdoms; Kumbi falls to Almoravids
1087	Soninke recapture Kumbi
1099	The first Crusade reaches the Holy Land
1203	Sosso leader Sumanguru captures Kumbi
1235	Sundiata defeats Sumanguru at Kirina; kingdom of Mali formed
1255	Sundiata dies
1279	Mongol empire at its height
1312	Mansa Musa becomes king of Mali
1324	Mansa Musa makes a pilgrimage to Mecca
1337	Mansa Musa dies
1347	A deadly plague wipes out one third of Europe's population
1368	Ming dynasty comes into power in China
1375	Earliest map of West Africa

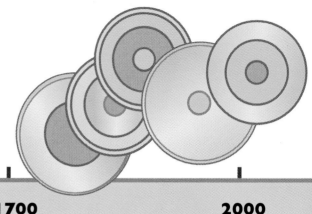

1400

1700

2000

1400s Aztecs dominate Central America

1414 East African ambassadors visit the Chinese emperor

1433 Tuareg chief Akil captures Timbuktu

1450 West African kingdom of Benin at its height

1453 Turks capture Constantinople; Europeans seek new trade routes

1454 Printing press invented in Germany

1464 Sunni Ali Ber becomes king of Songhay

1471 Portuguese build a trading fort on Guinea coast

1473 End of siege of Jenne; most of Mali now in Songhay empire

1492 Columbus arrives in the Americas; Sunni Ali Ber dies.

1493 Askia Mohammed Touré comes to power

1498 Vasco da Gama sails around Africa to India

1519 Ferdinand Magellan begins voyage around the world

1520 El-Kati writes *Tarikh al-Fettash*

1532 First shipment of African slaves to the Americas

1538 Askia Mohammed Touré dies

1543 Copernicus develops modern solar theory of planets revolving around the sun

1591 Songhay overthrown by Moroccan army, followed by the rise and fall of several lesser kingdoms

1607 British establish settlement at Jamestown, Virginia

1643 Louis XIV becomes king of France

1788 African Association formed

1805 Mungo Park traces course of River Niger

1826 Gordon Laing becomes first European to visit Timbuktu

1884 Imperial powers divide up Africa at the Berlin Congress

1894 France conquers Timbuktu; most of the western Sudan is annexed as French West Africa

1914 Ruins of Kumbi found at Kumbi Saleh; start of World War I

1939 Start of World War II

1960 Colonies of French West Africa gain independence

Ghana—The First Kingdom of West Africa

Ouagadou-Bida: The Sacred Serpent

Long ago, the ruler of the ancient kingdom of Ghana lived in the city of El Ghaba. The royal palace in El Ghaba was a mighty fortress with glass windows and great courtyards. Its myriad inner halls and rooms housed servants, soldiers, the king's family and relatives, princes from other regions, and a continuous stream of guests.

The king of Ghana ruled over a vast region and was fabulously wealthy. He had a trained army of 200,000 warriors. In the palace alone lived 1,000 horses in stalls as clean and richly appointed as any of its rooms. Each horse had a halter of silken rope and its own special mattress and was attended day and night by three servants.

When the king was ready to give audience to his people and listen to their complaints, a great drum was played, and its rhythms could be heard throughout the city. The king sat in a richly decorated pavilion surrounded by ten horses arrayed in gold cloth. Behind the king stood ten pages holding shields and gold-mounted swords. To his right stood the young princes of the empire, luxuriously clad in silk, with gold strands plaited into their hair. The governor of the city and his ministers sat on the ground in front of the king, and specially trained dogs wearing collars of silver and gold guarded the gate of the king's chamber.

Every evening the king sat on a balcony on a throne of gleaming red gold, surrounded by hundreds of slaves and thousands of his subjects. A huge fire of a thousand pieces of wood lit the scene, and with an imperial gesture, the king commanded the palace servants to bring forth food for the 10,000 people who dined with him each night.

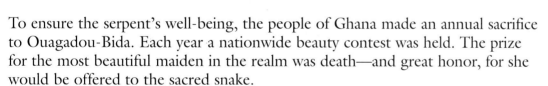

The king ruled supreme over the kingdom. His people enjoyed good health, happiness, peace, and prosperity. And all of this, so the people said, was given to the kingdom by the grace of the spirit serpent, Ouagadou-Bida (wah gah doo BEE dah).

Ouagadou-Bida lived in a cave in a sacred grove of trees just outside the city walls. This grove was fiercely guarded by priests. Intruders and nonbelievers who dared enter the sacred grove were never seen again. The king himself was allowed to enter the sacred grove on only two occasions—the day of his crowning and the day of his death, when he was buried in the royal tomb within the grove.

To ensure the serpent's well-being, the people of Ghana made an annual sacrifice to Ouagadou-Bida. Each year a nationwide beauty contest was held. The prize for the most beautiful maiden in the realm was death—and great honor, for she would be offered to the sacred snake.

One year the time for the sacrifice had arrived. The priests scoured the empire for a young girl beautiful enough to be offered to Ouagadou-Bida. At last, they selected the lovely Sia (SEE yah) from the nearby city of Kumbi, and preparations for the ceremony began. But as it happened, Sia was betrothed to a fearless warrior named

Amadou Sefedokote (AH mah doo se fe doh KOH tay). He loved Sia with all his heart and could not bear to see her die for the snake.

On the eve of the sacrifice, Amadou stole into the sacred grove and hid behind a tree. When Ouagadou-Bida emerged from the cave, Amadou drew his great sword and sliced off the snake's head. But Ouagadou-Bida had magical powers. His head flew far, far away, eventually landing outside the kingdom, in the town of Bambuk (bahm BOOK). Immediately the people of Bambuk found their pockets full of gold.

Ouagadou-Bida grew a new head, and the warrior Amadou severed it once more. Again the head flew through the air, landing this time in far-off Bure (boo RAY). At once, Bure's streets were filled with gold. Again and again, Amadou tried to kill the serpent with mighty thrusts of his sword. Each time, the snake's head flew off and landed in some far-off place, making it rich in gold.

At last, after Amadou had severed seven heads, Ouagadou-Bida's powers were exhausted. The spirit snake lay down and died. Amadou leaped onto a great white steed, snatched his lovely bride Sia from the sacrificial altar, and galloped away, never to be seen again.

The people of Ghana wept and cursed Amadou, for they knew that without Ouagadou-Bida their kingdom was doomed. The priests tried everything in their power to bring the snake back to life, but all their efforts failed. Ouagadou-Bida was dead.

Shortly afterward, the kingdom of Ghana suffered a terrible drought. The green and fertile lands dried up, and the cattle and goats died. Nothing would grow in the fields.

Terrified of the curse that had afflicted their land, the people fled. They took with them what few belongings they could and wandered as nomads. With the death of Ouagadou-Bida, the great kingdom of Ghana had come to an end.

Ghana's Early History

The legend of Ouagadou-Bida is an ancient story, handed down orally from generation to generation for over a thousand years. It is still told today among the modern Soninke (soh-NIHN ke) people, the descendants of those who lived so long ago in the kingdom of Ghana. But how much of the legend is true? How did Ghana rise to power in the first

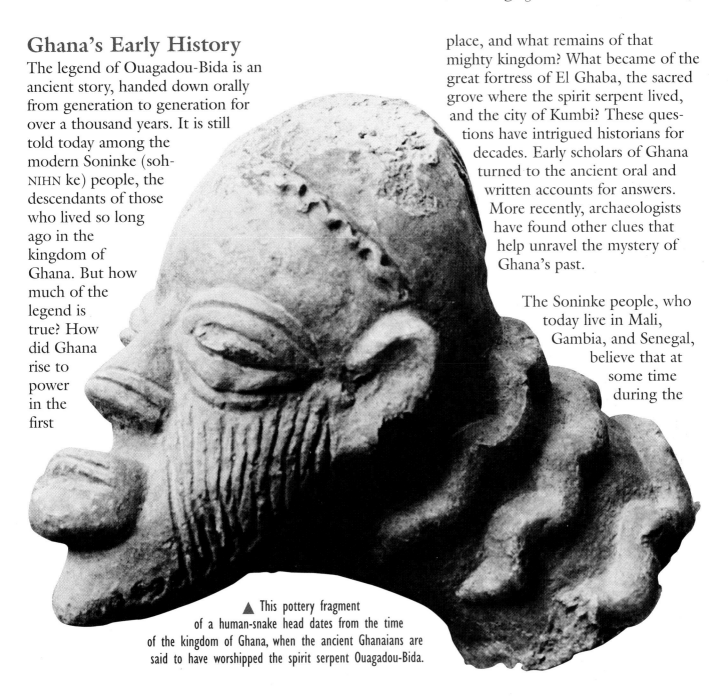

▲ This pottery fragment of a human-snake head dates from the time of the kingdom of Ghana, when the ancient Ghanaians are said to have worshipped the spirit serpent Ouagadou-Bida.

place, and what remains of that mighty kingdom? What became of the great fortress of El Ghaba, the sacred grove where the spirit serpent lived, and the city of Kumbi? These questions have intrigued historians for decades. Early scholars of Ghana turned to the ancient oral and written accounts for answers. More recently, archaeologists have found other clues that help unravel the mystery of Ghana's past.

The Soninke people, who today live in Mali, Gambia, and Senegal, believe that at some time during the second or third century A.D. their ancestors settled in the wide valley between the Senegal River to the west and the Niger River to the east. This area was part of a vast territory that the Arabs called the *Bilad es Sudan,* the "land of the blacks." Over time the region came to be known as the Sudan.

The Soninke territory, located in the western Sudan, commanded an isolated oasis along an important trade route that was thousands of miles long. This oasis, historians believe, probably became the site of the city of Kumbi. The trade route began in the northwestern areas bordering the Sahara, crossed the desert, and continued south toward what is now the Gulf of Guinea and east toward present-day Chad. The Soninke imposed heavy taxes on merchants traveling this route and thus amassed considerable wealth. It is not clear, however, how the Soninke built their resources into what is the first recorded kingdom of the western Sudan.

There are several theories about the founders of the kingdom of Ghana. Some historians have suggested that

leadership may have come from a powerful tribe of Jews who had been driven from a Roman colony in the north and had migrated south. Others credit the Berbers, a North African people, with founding the ruling dynasty of the kingdom. These historians found it difficult to believe that Africans were able to develop an empire on their own, but there is little evidence for their theories. It is far more likely that the Soninke themselves founded the kingdom of Ghana. It is said that in about A.D. 700 a Soninke chief succeeded in uniting the Soninke people under his leadership and may even have founded the city of Kumbi.

This chief must have been a great warrior and diplomat. He belonged to the royal clan of Ouagadou, and the Soninke first named their kingdom after this royal family. The chief was known as the *kaya maghan* (kai yah mah GAHN), "king of the gold," and as *ghana,* "war chief." Over time the land of Ouagadou became known as Ghana.

The People of Ghana
The Soninke people were a group of related tribes who all spoke the language

In 1957, the Gold Coast, which had belonged to the British, became the first African colony to achieve its independence. Although it bore little geographical relation to ancient Ghana, the Gold Coast was renamed Ghana in honor of the first great West African kingdom.

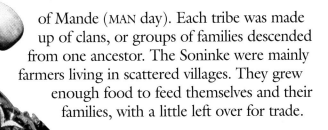

of Mande (MAN day). Each tribe was made up of clans, or groups of families descended from one ancestor. The Soninke were mainly farmers living in scattered villages. They grew enough food to feed themselves and their families, with a little left over for trade.

Each clan was headed by the oldest male member. Many clans had specific occupations. For example, men of the Kante (KAN tay) clan specialized in metalworking and were professional blacksmiths, while the kings and heads of provinces came from the Sisse (SEE say) family. Other clans made a living by hunting wild game or by fishing and providing transport along the many rivers.

Along the important rivers and trade routes were the larger towns and cities, where many thousands of people lived. They bought their food from the farmers and concentrated instead on crafts, such as making tools and jewelry or weaving cloth.

Europeans call African ethnic groups "tribes," whether referring to the 17 million Igbo people of Nigeria or to a village of a few hundred individuals. Like Native Americans and other peoples, Africans who share a common language and culture prefer being referred to as members of a nation rather than members of a tribe.

◀ Magic talismans like these, known as *gris-gris* (gree gree), may have been fashioned and traded by craftsmen in the cities of ancient Ghana. The leather pouches are filled with crushed roots, herbs, leaves, and bark. They function as charms to ward off evil.

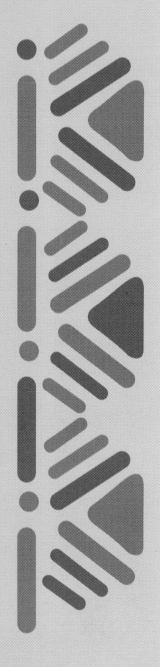

Many city dwellers were traders, exchanging local goods for those brought from places thousands of miles away.

Soninke families, like others throughout the Sudan, were made up of many people, including a man and his wife or wives and all their children and relatives, both close and distant. Often, several generations of a clan might live in one compound. To the children in a family, all adult men were "fathers" and all adult women were "mothers," while all children were "sisters" and "brothers."

Living with a wealthier clan might also be a number of servants and even slaves, who were usually war captives. Most clans employed their own historians, called *griots* (GREE-ohz) whose job it was to memorize and hand down the family stories in songs and ballads.

The Soninke people celebrated the seasons and their religious beliefs in many rituals and forms of song, dance, and prayers. Like many other African people, they believed in a Creator or High God who was responsible for everything. They also believed that everything living and nonliving was possessed by a spirit—perhaps that of a recently dead relative, a long-dead ancestor, or a spirit of nature. These spirits could do good or evil to a family or individual, and the Soninke carefully performed the necessary rituals to keep the spirits content. They also wore certain charms as protection. Priests, who were thought to be magicians, conducted the religious ceremonies. Today most Soninke people are Muslims or Christians, but there are still those who cling to the old beliefs or practice them alongside their other beliefs.

The Salt-Gold Monopoly

Camel caravans crossing the Sahara brought to Ghana many goods. These included copper, dried fruit, and cowrie shells, which were used as a medium of exchange. The most important commodity carried by the caravans, however, was salt, an essential nutrient in the human diet. Salt was desperately needed—in fact, craved—by the people of Wangara, who lived in the intensely hot savannah to the south of Ghana, where no salt was available. In exchange for the salt, the Wangara provided a seemingly endless supply of gold, panned from the flood plains and beds of their rivers.

Merchants on the salt-gold route had to pass through Ghana. The Ghanaians thus acted as middlemen or agents in the trade of salt for gold and collected huge taxes on these and all other commodities.

The Latin word for salt is *sal*. Roman soldiers received salt as part of their pay, which was called a *salarium*—hence the word *salary*. A really good soldier was "worth his salt."

The salt was mined at a desolate place called Taghaza (tah GAH zah) in the desert far to the northeast of Ghana, in present-day Algeria. An Arab traveler and historian named Ibn Battuta (ihb ihn bah TOO tah), who passed through Taghaza in the mid-fourteenth century, described the place in his

Blocks of salt from the northern Sahara are transported across the desert to markets in the south, like this one on the Niger River. ▼

Covering 200 miles of desert in a week, regular camel caravans brought products from Europe and North Africa across the Sahara to the great
market cities of the western Sudan. On the return trip, camels
took products from the south for trade in the north. Camel
caravans still cross the Sahara today.

Much of the gold traded in ancient Ghana and areas farther east was made into coins under the imprint of Muslim sultans in Morocco, Tunisia, and Egypt. The first mint on the ancient trade route from Ghana north to Morocco was at Sijilmasa. The coins, called dinars, had a standard weight of 4.233 g (.148 oz). This weight was called a mictal. In eleventh-century Cairo (Egypt), a lower-class working family could live on 2 dinars a month. A slave cost about 20 dinars, and a good female cook could cost 100 dinars or more!

journal as follows: "an unattractive village, . . . its houses and mosques [Muslim temples] are built of blocks of salt, roofed with camel skins. There are no trees there, nothing but sand. In the sand is a salt mine; they dig for the salt and find it in thick slabs, lying one on top of the other."

Right through the sixteenth century, salt was mined in this way in Taghaza. The inhabitants of Taghaza were slaves, owned by Arab merchants. These merchants came to Taghaza from the distant inland cities of Sijilmasa (sih jihl MAH sah) and Marrakesh on the northern borders of the Sahara, in what is today Morocco. In these cities the merchants bought European, Arabian, and Egyptian goods that had been transported by donkeys all the way from the fertile Mediterranean coast. The goods were then transferred to camels and carried across the Sahara. In Taghaza, the camel caravans added salt to their loads and took it south to the main markets of Ghana and to the Wangara. African porters carried some goods even farther south, to markets on the Gulf of Guinea. From Ghana, the camels returned across the Sahara laden with kola nuts, hides, leather goods, ivory, gold, and slaves.

Although the location of Taghaza is known, the mystery of the whereabouts of the Wangara gold mines has never been solved. The location of the mines was kept secret by all the kings of Ghana, and by the Wangara themselves, who knew that their prosperity depended on the gold. Greedy mer-

Amazingly early in human history, people began to dig for salt. A 1,000-year-old mine in Poland still holds the giant, toothed wheels and huge staircases once used in mining, all surrounded by glittering salt. This mine is now a dance hall! The city of Detroit, Michigan, is situated over the hollowed-out shafts of a salt mine. In Russia, minerals in the walls of an ancient salt mine are said to help people with allergies, and the mine is now a clinic. One of the world's oldest trade routes is the Via Salaria, or Salt Road. It connected the port of Ostia on Italy's western shore with Rome and the Adriatic Sea.

◀ Solid gold earrings, similar to those worn by the women of ancient Mali 1,000 years ago, are still worn today by women of the region.

chants once tried to find the mines by capturing a Wangara man. Rather than reveal the secret, he pined away and died. This treachery caused a three-year halt in the gold trade. The Wangara resumed trading only because of their desperate need for salt.

Wherever it came from, gold was so plentiful in Ghana that even the king's hitching post was said to have been a 60-pound gold nugget, which would be worth more than $300,000 today! The kings of Ghana understood that to maintain its value, they had to control the supply of gold on the open market. They thus declared that all gold nuggets found anywhere in the kingdom belonged to the king. This way, gold nuggets were effectively removed from trade, leaving only the gold dust for the market.

The salt-gold trade was the lifeblood of the kingdom. It was carried out in a most extraordinary fashion called silent barter. The Wangara chose a trading site on the banks of a river. To this site, the merchants from Ghana brought salt, as well as animal skins, ivory, kola nuts, wool, silk, cotton, dates, figs, and other goods. Each merchant laid his bars of salt on the ground, with his goods nearby. The Wangara remained out of sight. The traders beat their drums to announce that the market was open. Then they retired several miles from the site.

The Wangara came by boat to inspect the goods. Next to each pile of salt, they laid a bag of gold dust. It is said that the Wangara valued the salt equally with their gold and exchanged it pound for pound. They beat drums to signal their withdrawal from sight and the Ghanaians would return. If the Ghanaians were satisfied with the trade, they collected their gold and left. If not, they withdrew again. Hoping for a better price, they left everything in place. This continued until the deal was finally completed. Then the merchants sounded the great drums again to signal the end of trade and departed. This method worked well for centuries and was an excellent way of maintaining the secrecy of the gold mines while allowing people who did not speak the same language to trade with one another.

The Tax System

The king collected taxes on every single trade item that entered the country. For each load of salt coming from the north into the city of Kumbi, for example, a merchant had to pay one gold coin, called a dinar. A dinar was defined as the weight of 72 grains of barley, or about one sixth of an ounce (almost 5 grams).

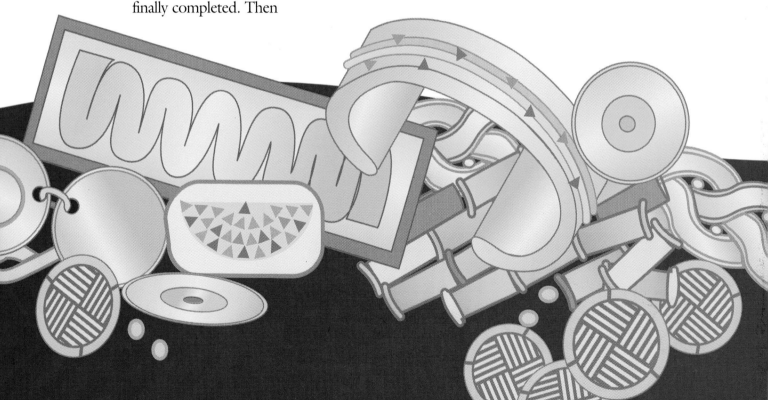

The merchant had to pay another two dinars to take that load of salt out of Kumbi, to the south. Thus each time a load of salt passed through the kingdom, the king was three dinars, or half an ounce (15 grams) of gold, richer. The tax on every load of copper was about five eighths of an ounce of gold, and general merchandise was taxed at one ounce of gold per load.

Merchants did not complain about the taxes because the money raised was used to maintain a peaceful, prosperous kingdom through which they could travel in safety. Gold paid for the efficient government and the huge army, which protected its borders and trade routes. Gold paid

for the upkeep of the capital city and major markets. Merchants felt safe in Ghana. The guarantee of safety attracted more merchants and more trade. Doing business in Ghana was a profitable and pleasurable experience.

Gold also had a practical use based on its value. It could be made into coins and used as currency. This coin was minted in Sijilmasa in 1075. The name on the coin is that of Abu Bakr, the Almoravid leader who sacked Kumbi in 1067.

Meteors contain iron that can be hammered into shape. Soft iron is also a byproduct in the manufacture of metals such as gold and copper. Useful for ornaments and jewelry, it is not hard enough for weapons or tools. Hard iron is made through a very complex process of smelting, heating, and hammering. The secrets of iron making probably traveled across the Sahara from Morocco and from Meroë, on the Nile River, where iron working was highly developed long before the birth of Christ. Iron working required plenty of wood to fuel the smelters' fires. Iron foundries often closed down when the available wood was used up.

scissors

knife blade

sickle

Iron Tools Excavated from Kumbi Saleh

The Iron Warriors

The trade in gold and salt made the empire of Ghana rich, but it was iron that provided the army with superior weapons and enabled the kingdom to conquer its neighbors and expand its borders.

Iron ore was and still is plentiful in many parts of the Sudan and has possibly been mined and worked in the area for 2,000 years or more. The availability of iron brought great and lasting change to life in West Africa.

Iron was easier to obtain than other metals, such as copper or bronze, which had been widely used earlier. Tools made of iron were stronger, sharper, and more durable than those made of wood, copper, stone, bone, or bronze—the materials commonly used elsewhere. Iron tools made farming easier and raised the standard of agriculture. Iron spearheads, lances, knives, and swords were far superior to the wooden staves or bows and arrows of neighboring peoples.

With plenty of food, an abundance of precious gold, an extensive trade network, and a well-equipped army, the early Soninke had everything they needed to develop a powerful empire.

The Arab Invasion

Until the eighth century, Ghana was unknown outside of West and Northwest Africa. But events far to the north, along the Mediterranean and Atlantic coasts, would eventually change life in ancient Ghana forever.

By A.D. 681, Arab conquerors from the Middle East had swept west along the Mediterranean coast to Tangier, in Morocco. They were Muslims, followers of the prophet Mohammed,

Among the iron tools found in excavations at Kumbi Saleh were a curved knife blade and a sickle. A pair of iron scissors found at the site is one of the oldest known to exist.

who had founded the religion of Islam (see Chapter 3). They believed in the one God, Allah, and conquered not only to add new territories to their lands but also to convert all "infidels," or nonbelievers, to Islam.

In Morocco, the Arabs heard of a great prize farther south—an African kingdom with a seemingly inexhaustible supply of gold! They decided to send part of their forces south, following the caravan routes across the Sahara to find the land of gold. Elsewhere, the Arabs had easily conquered lands and people. But in Ghana they met their match in the 200,000-strong Ghanaian army. They were astonished as they faced 40,000 archers and as many horsemen and infantry, well equipped with chain-mail armor, spears, lances, and bows and arrows.

The Arabs failed to conquer Ghana, but many of them decided to settle there. They established close connections between the Arab and the African worlds, and business prospered as never before. New goods, such as silk, swords, and books, now crossed the Sahara.

Not only goods wound along the age-old trade routes. Along with the new immigrants came new ideas. The Arabs brought with them the religion of Islam. They brought learning in mathematics, science, and architecture that was the most advanced in the world, far exceeding the level of knowledge in Europe at the time. And they brought Arabic writing. For the first time, West African stories, chronicles, legends, and fables could be written down.

The Early Written History

The first written records of Ghana were compiled in Arabic in A.D. 970 by the Arab traveler Ibn Haukal (ihb ihn HOU kahl). By that time, Ghana was already an immensely rich and prosperous empire. There were no formally marked boundaries, but scholars have established that at the height of its power Ghana controlled territories from the Atlantic Ocean in the west to the great bend of the Niger River in the east, and from the Sahara in the north to the lands south of the Niger.

Ibn Haukal claimed that the king of Ghana at the time was "the richest king in the world because of his gold." A century later, in 1067, the famed Arab scholar El-Bekri confirmed this. His monumental *Book of Roads and Kingdoms* provides us with many details about the cities, social life, customs, trade, and government of Ghana.

El-Bekri never set foot in Ghana. He lived in Córdoba, Spain, and relied on the reports of caravan leaders, merchants, and travelers. Later, in about A.D. 1520, a Muslim Soninke called El-Kati compiled the history of Ghana in a book titled *Tarikh al-Fettash* (tah reek el fet ASH). But El-Bekri's accounts were the first to inform

The history of Ghana and other kingdoms in the western Sudan was recorded by various Arab historians. This section of the *Tarikh es Sudan*, written by Es-Sadi in 1656, provided an account of the growth of cities in the region. Arabic is read from right to left. ▼

the outside world that a great kingdom existed in the interior of West Africa, a kingdom that could rival any that Europe had ever known.

Political Organization

Arab traders and travelers were surprised at the immense wealth of Ghana, which was even greater than they had been led to believe. But the kingdom's well-organized system of government astonished them even more.

From El-Bekri and other Arab sources, we know that the king of Ghana was the "father" of all the Soninke people. He was their religious leader, the chief of their army, the highest justice, and the leader of the empire. In fact, the people thought of the king as a god. One of the king's main tasks was to act as a judge and hear his people's cases and petitions. Each day the king would tour the city, stopping now and then to hear complaints or make judicial decisions on the spot. He was always accompanied by several elders, musicians, town criers, and drummers, who made so much noise that no one could miss the daily event. The king also held court in his palace. There was

a lower court and a higher court of appeal, but in the end the king had the final word.

Below the king a hierarchy of officers helped rule the land. A governor ruled the capital city of Kumbi. Lesser governors managed the outer regions of the kingdom. When new areas were conquered, their leaders were allowed to remain in power as long as they stayed loyal to the great *kaya maghan*, "king of the gold." To ensure this loyalty, their sons and heirs apparent had to join the king's court, where they could be closely watched.

The Soninke believed that the king would continue to rule in the afterlife, so his power extended even after death. When a king died, a wooden house was built for the body. He was laid on a bed, surrounded by his weapons, clothes, food, drink, and anything else he might need in the next world. Living slaves who would serve the dead king were also sealed inside the tomb, which was then covered over with earth.

A king was not succeeded by his own son, but by his sister's son. This system of succession is called matrilineal, because it is based on the mother's line. It guarantees that the king's family line is handed down genetically.

The Twin Cities

The cities mentioned in the legend, El Ghaba and Kumbi, actually existed. El-Bekri was the first to give detailed descriptions of them. The two towns were located about six miles apart on a plain and were separated by a long, straight avenue, lined with houses of wood and stone.

The city of Kumbi was inhabited mainly by Arab and Berber merchants. These people were Muslims, and El-Bekri notes that there were no less than 12 mosques in Kumbi. Each mosque had its own paid staff; its chief minister, the *imam* (ee MAHM); and scholars of the Quran (ko RAHN), or Koran, the holy book of Islam. Surrounding the town, according to El-Bekri, were "wells of sweet water from which they drink and near which they grow vegetables."

Kumbi's market was reputedly the busiest in West Africa. Men, women, and children went about their daily business amid the clatter of horses' hooves and the snorting

of camels. The Soninke people were skilled at many crafts, and the market rang to the sound of hammers and anvils. Ironsmiths made weapons and tools; goldsmiths and coppersmiths made jewelry. There were also potters, weavers, and leather workers. The Moroccan leather goods still popular today originated in Ghana. And, of course, there was the bustling slave market.

Cattle, sheep, honey, wheat, raisins, dried fruit, ivory, and even pearls could also be bought in Kumbi. These goods were brought from the farthest reaches of the kingdom, from the lands around the Mediterranean and from distant Egypt and Arabia. There were red and blue blouses imported from Spain and handsome robes from Morocco. And everything was paid for in gold dust. It was indeed an energetic, cosmopolitan place—an African crossroads of people and goods that was a source of wonder to travelers for centuries.

El Ghaba was a different place altogether. El-Bekri reports that when the king gave audience, he and the entire court wore ceremonial robes of cotton, brocade, or silk. The

Muslims present clapped their hands quietly. Non-Muslims fell to their knees and poured earth over their heads. This was their way of greeting the king.

El-Bekri also writes that "around the king's town are woods where live the sorcerers of the people, the men in charge of the religious cult. These woods are guarded and no unauthorized person can enter them." The name *El Ghaba* actually means "forest." Just as the legend relates, it was believed that the spirit serpent, Ouagadou-Bida, lived in a sacred grove in the woods outside El Ghaba. And it was in this grove that the annual sacrifice of a beautiful maiden was made to the serpent. Should anything happen to Ouagadou-Bida, the people thought, the kingdom was sure to perish. Unauthorized entry into the grove was punishable by death. El-Bekri also mentions that there were prisons in the grove, from which no one ever emerged alive.

Why did the capital of Ghana consist of two cities, each so different from

Long before the Europeans established the slave trade with the Americas, Arabs and Africans practiced slavery. It was an ugly but profitable business.

In Ghana the slave trade was a major source of income. The city of Kumbi supported one of the largest slave markets along the trans-Saharan caravan routes. Slaves were usually captured from conquered territories. They were sometimes bought by wealthy Africans and remained in Ghana. Often, however, they were sold to Arab merchants and taken across the Sahara to markets in the north. From there, slaves might end up in any of the North African or Arabian countries or even in Europe.

Most slaves were trained as bodyguards and soldiers or worked in households. Many worked as salt or metal miners or on plantations or building projects. If a

the other? El-Bekri comments that "the king's interpreters, his treasurer and the majority of his ministers, are Muslims." In other words, although the kings of Ghana were non-Muslim, they clearly showed great respect for Muslim learning and diplomats and relied on Muslim trade. But the Ghanaian rulers preferred to practice their own beliefs within the safety of their mighty walls. In El Ghaba, they were cautious of foreigners who might plot to overthrow the monarchy or rob the palace vaults of their vast treasures in gold.

All this splendor and activity was chronicled by the early historians. Yet by the end of the thirteenth century, the kingdom of Ghana had ceased to exist, and the twin cities of Kumbi and El Ghaba seemed to have disappeared. It was not until 1914—some 700 years later—that a French archaeologist named Bonnel de Mézières (metz ee AIR) located the possible site of Kumbi at a place called Kumbi Saleh (sah LE), on today's border between Mali and Mauritania. Ten miles away, the ruins of another town were uncovered, known to

female slave bore her master a child, it was his duty to take care of her and her children. After his death, she became a free woman.

There were many laws governing the treatment of slaves, who were often regarded as members of a household. Some were educated at the expense of their masters and even became governors or advisors to their rulers. Nevertheless, slaves were at the mercy of their masters, were often treated harshly, and suffered the anguish of being uprooted from their homelands and separated from their families.

TRADE

the local people as Ghanata. Could Ghanata be the lost city of El Ghaba, home of the fabled serpent, Ouagadou-Bida? There is as yet no proof, but perhaps, in time, this mystery also will be solved.

The Fall of the Empire

The legend says that the death of Ouagadou-Bida caused the fall of Ghana. History tells a different but no less tragic story.

When El-Bekri wrote about Ghana in 1067, the kingdom was at the height of its power. Only ten years later, however, it began a headlong fall from which it would never recover. In 1030, a Muslim preacher named Abdullah ibn Yasin (ab DUL luh ihb ihn ya SEEN), founded a militant sect dedicated to spreading the purest possible form of Islam. The sect was based at a secret monastery on an island off the Atlantic coast. When Ibn Yasin's followers numbered 1,000, he named them *el morabetin* (el moh RAH be teen), "men of the monastery." Western historians call this sect the Almoravids.

By 1042, nearly 30,000 men had rallied to Ibn Yasin's call.

These desert warriors were extremely skilled military tacticians and were willing to die for their faith. Heavily armed and mounted on camels and horses, they raged through the western Sudan in terrifying hordes, waging their *jihad* (jee HAHD), or holy war, wherever they went. Their battle cry was to convert the kingdom's nonbelievers to Islam. They also had an eye on the lucrative gold trade.

In 1067, after ten heroic years of resistance, the city of Kumbi finally fell to the Almoravids, who killed all who refused to convert to Islam. But now the Almoravids had to deal with a kingdom in uproar. In Ghana, there were many rebellious subkingdoms that had been waiting for an opportunity to break free from the Soninke stranglehold. This was their chance. One revolt after another broke out. But the Almoravids lacked the huge military force, the well-organized government, and the spending power that was available to the kings of Ghana. The Almoravids' hold on Kumbi weakened, and after their leader's death in 1087, the Soninke were able to reclaim their throne and rebuild the city.

But the revived Soninke rule was also brief. Thirty-three years of battling the Almoravids had shattered the central power of the Ghanaian kings. Many smaller provinces of the empire had declared their independence and become separate kingdoms. One of these was Sosso; its leader, the fierce warrior Sumanguru, briefly rose to power. In 1203, he captured Kumbi, claimed all the territories of the ancient empire, and enslaved its inhabitants. But Sumanguru was fighting a losing battle. The vital trade routes through Ghana had become extremely dangerous, and as a result the Muslim merchants had simply packed up and left. With the loss of trade—the lifeblood of the empire—the kingdom of Ghana began to crumble.

In addition to all this, a terrible drought descended on the kingdom. Rainfall was poor, and crops failed. The people were already suffering from poverty and starvation in their war-ridden kingdom. Just as the legend of Ouagadou-Bida tells us, they began to move away in search of more peaceful lands. After more than 500 years, the kingdom of Ghana was now a mere shadow of its former self. Meanwhile, new forces to the south were growing in power. By the mid-thirteenth century, the once-great empire of Ghana had vanished.

2

A Good Place for a Kingdom

As was the case in kingdoms that appeared and disappeared elsewhere in the world, the rise and fall of ancient Ghana was no accident. Nor was Ghana the only kingdom to arise from the soils of the western Sudan. From the third century A.D. to the beginning of the colonial period in the nineteenth century, one powerful kingdom after another blossomed and died in the region. What was it about the western Sudan that encouraged the development of these great African empires?

The Sahel

Ancient Ghana and other kingdoms that arose in the western Sudan developed in the region known today as the *Sahel* (sah HEL). The word *sahel* means "shore" in Arabic. If the Sahara is thought of as an ocean, then the Sahel is aptly named.

The Sahel is a strip of land ranging from 200 to 800 km (124 to 496 mi) wide and stretching 6,000 km (3,700 mi) across Africa, from the Atlantic coast of Senegal and Mauritania in the west through Mali, Niger, Chad, and the Sudan before it veers south through Ethiopia, Somalia, and northern Kenya. The Sahel is bordered to the north by the Sahara and to the south by tropical forests. Three great rivers—the Senegal, Niger, and Nile—cut through the Sahel at approximately 1,000 km (620 mi) intervals. They nurture vital strips of agriculture along their banks.

Water is life. In the Sahel, water is central to the social, cultural, and economic life of the people. Just as it has for centuries, rainfall rather than politics dictates the way of life of the 50 to 60 million people living in the Sahel today.

The annual rainfall varies from one area to the next in the Sahel, and the region can be divided into three long strips according to levels of precipitation. The narrowest strip borders the Sahara and receives only 50 to 200 mm (2 to 8 in) of rain each year. Here, agriculture is impossible, and nomadic pastoralists (people who keep herds of domestic

Animals and people rest at this nomadic camp in the northern Sahel. Mats, cooking pots, sleeping mats, bed poles, clothes, and sacks of food and other supplies are just some of the possessions that camels and donkeys carry for their owners as the nomads wander the lands bordering the Sahara. ▼

At the time that Ghana was rising to power in the western Sudan, the French king Charles the Great, or Charlemagne, was forging the Holy Roman Empire in Europe. The empire Charlemagne established lasted over a thousand years, from 800 to 1806. The Mayas of Central America were building a flourishing empire in the same period, with huge cities dominated by massive temples. And by the thirteenth century, the Mongols of central Asia ruled an empire stretching almost from the Baltic Sea to the Pacific Ocean and from the Persian Gulf to the Arctic Circle.

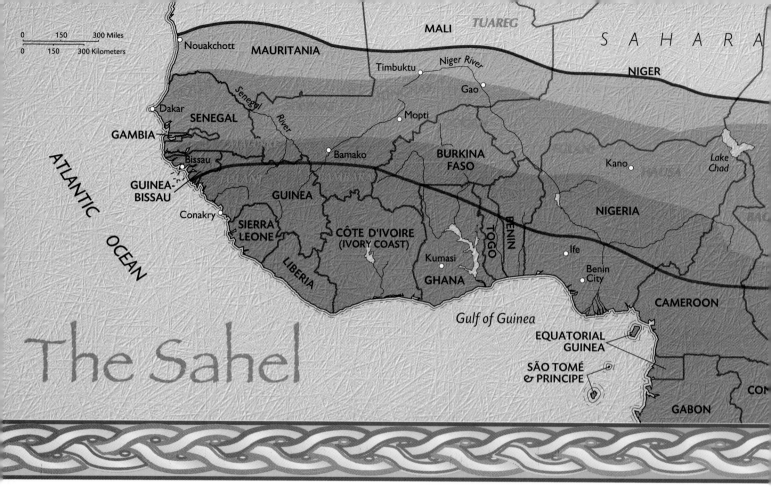

The Sahel

animals) in this area live today much as they did 2,000 years ago. The Tuareg (too AH reg), for example, move between Algeria, Mali, and Niger with their herds of camels, sheep, and goats.

The central and widest strip of the Sahel is savannah, which can receive up to 800 mm (32 in) of rain each year. Many different peoples, such as the Soninke, the Songhay, the Dogon, the Fulani, and the Hausa, inhabit this region. Some, like the Fulani, include both full nomads, such as the WoDaaBe (woh DAH be), and settled "agro-pastoralists," who grow crops and keep animals. Others are farmers, living in permanent villages. Along the rivers, people also fish.

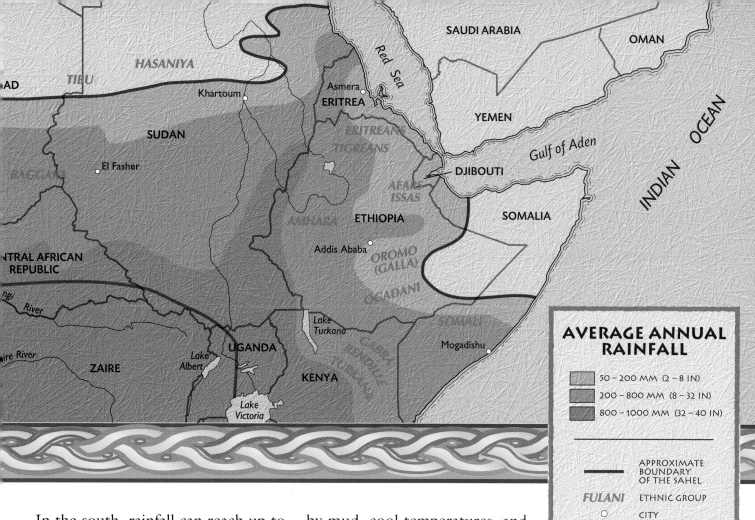

HASANIYA

TIBU

AD

CHAD

SUDAN

Khartoum

El Fasher

BAGGARA

NTRAL AFRICAN
REPUBLIC

ngi
River

ire River

ZAIRE

UGANDA

Lake
Albert

Lake
Victoria

SAUDI ARABIA

OMAN

Red Sea

Asmera

ERITREA

ERITREANS

TIGREANS

YEMEN

Gulf of Aden

DJIBOUTI

INDIAN OCEAN

AFAR
ISSAS

AMHARA

ETHIOPIA

SOMALIA

Addis Ababa

OROMO
(GALLA)

OGADANI

Lake
Turkana

GABRA
RENDILLE
TURKANA

SOMALI

KENYA

Mogadishu

**AVERAGE ANNUAL
RAINFALL**

   50 – 200 MM (2 – 8 IN)

   200 – 800 MM (8 – 32 IN)

   800 – 1000 MM (32 – 40 IN)

─────── APPROXIMATE
BOUNDARY
OF THE SAHEL

FULANI   ETHNIC GROUP

  o   CITY

In the south, rainfall can reach up to 1,000 mm (40 in) annually. Cattle, especially the long-horned Zebu variety, thrive best here and are preferred by southern pastoralists such as the Baggara of Sudan and Chad.

During the rainy season, which usually extends from July to October, southern pastoralists are driven north by mud, cool temperatures, and the deadly tsetse (TSEHT see) fly, which causes sleeping sickness. Northern pastoralists, however, move south, seeking greener pastures. During this season, the watering holes of the central Sahel become a meeting ground for different groups of people, often with huge herds of livestock.

The entire Sahel, sandwiched as it is between the desert and the forest, has always been subjected to severe changes in climate. Rain may fail entirely, causing periods of severe drought during which untold thousands of people and livestock starve to death, as they did from 1968 to 1973. As the legend of Ouagadou-Bida tells us, one such drought followed the downfall of the kingdom of Ghana, causing its people to seek new pastures. Drought can also lead to cattle rustling and fierce tribal skirmishes over watering and grazing rights. To make matters worse, when the rains do come, they often fall in torrents, washing away tons of soil. In 1988, for example, the city of Khartoum in the Sudan received almost all of its annual rainfall in a single night!

Temperatures in the Sahel during the day are usually very high, with almost

Too much rain can be as disastrous as too little. Here, a Fulani farmer in Niger examines his millet crop, which has been destroyed by torrential downpours.
▼

Cattle graze scrub grass on a farm in the southern Sahel ▶

In 1960 about 90 percent of Sahelians were farmers or pastoralists. Today this figure has shrunk to about 75 percent. In a process called desertification, the ongoing drought is extending the Sahara gradually southward and making it more and more difficult to grow crops. Rural people now frequently abandon their land and flock to the cities to find work. Today about 25 percent of Sahelians live in cities, and the number is growing rapidly.

zero humidity except near the rivers and coasts. For this reason, most of the landscape consists of wide, flat plains of acacia (uh KAY shuh) scrub and tough grasses, the few plants that can survive there. In the dry season the land is often scoured by searing, dust-laden winds. And every so often, plagues of locusts descend to destroy in hours what it has taken years to grow.

From Nomads to Kings

Like Stone Age people all over the world, people living in West Africa some 20,000 years ago hunted game and lived on fruit, nuts, roots, and berries that they gathered during their wanderings. Between 8000 and 4000 B.C., however, the climate became much wetter. The Sahara became a region of flowing rivers and grassy valleys, stretching from the bend of the Niger River to North Africa, east to the Nile and the lakes of East Africa, and south to include the Sahel. Crocodiles, hippopotamuses, and fish were plentiful. People hunted them skillfully with bone-headed harpoons, hooks and lines, and even fishing nets.

With abundant food available, there was no need to wander. People could settle in villages and develop crafts such as boat building, basketry, and pottery. Some became experienced pastoralists, tending large herds of cattle, sheep, and goats.

Around 4000 B.C., however, the Sahara began to dry out. No one knows why. But the edges of lakes retreated, and the flow of rivers declined. Over the centuries the desert spread steadily outward. Fishing and hunting could no longer provide enough food for the people who had made the Sahara their home. They had probably always gathered the grains of wild grasses for food. Now they learned how to cultivate and develop these grasses, which were varieties of sorghum, millet, and rice, all of which are grown in the region to this day.

As the Sahara continued to dry out, different ways of life became established in its various regions. By 600 B.C., the Sahara had become the desert we know today. Its sandy wastes were inhabited by nomadic pastoralists. But south of the desert, where the climate remained moist, farming became permanently established.

In the Sahelian steppe, a nomadic woman and child find shade in a simple shelter made of poles and mats. Inside, she places her bed, her valuable calabashes, and her mortar and pestle for grinding millet.

The Soninke people had their origins in this southernmost region. Their ancestors soon learned to use iron for tools and weapons. They also traded for horses from the nomads to the north.

These nomads probably posed a serious threat to the early Soninke. In times of drought, they would raid the villages to the south in search of water and pastures for their herds, and grain and other food for themselves. Possibly they captured slaves to cook for them and tend their animals. To protect themselves against these raids, the communities of African farmers in the south had to join forces. They needed to choose powerful war leaders. Perhaps these leaders were the first rulers of the loose federation of states that eventually became the kingdom of Ghana.

Forging Kingdoms

In the western Sudan, there were many incentives for the growth of kingdoms, which were political units in which many small states were governed by one ruler. Africans in the western Sudan and, indeed, over much of the continent had very strong ties to the land. Farming families inherited land through generations, and even distant relatives could claim rights to ancestral land. Nomads and pastoralists also claimed ancestral grazing grounds. This hereditary system is known as communalism. Certain professions, such as metalworking or weaving, were also inherited within families, who fiercely guarded their rights to these activities.

In the rural areas, government was simple: The head, or patriarch, of the family was the boss. But many people

Many rock paintings located along distinct routes, or "tracks," in the Sahara show two-wheeled chariots drawn by small horses. About the size of a Shetland pony, these tiny horses had come to the Sahara via Asia and Egypt around 1000 B.C. They could draw a chariot with a driver weighing 75 kg (165 lb) at about 38 km (24 mi) per hour over short distances.

As the Sahara dried out, the horse was gradually replaced by the camel, which was introduced from Asia in about the third century A.D. A camel can carry a load of 125 to 150 kg (275–330 lb) and travel up to 150 km (93 mi) in a day. It can go without water for several days and can survive on the sparse desert vegetation. The camel enabled traders to move faster over greater distances. It served as a beast of burden but also transported soldiers to war.

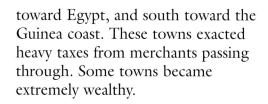

lived in towns and cities. There, government was more complicated, because there were more people to control. An overlord, who was rather like a mayor, was needed to make communal decisions. He had help from soldiers, police, and various government assistants. Local people were not given these jobs, because of the possibility of family quarrels. It was easier to fill these jobs with independent people from the outside, who had no family claims. Slaves served this purpose well.

Slaves were usually captives from other regions. As city populations grew, so did the lord's power. He needed more and more slaves for his armies and work forces. To get more slaves, he had to conquer more lands. Thus, cities eventually became city-states or the capitals of small states.

With commodities such as gold, salt, iron, and food in surplus, market towns like Audoghast (OU doh gast) and Kumbi and centers farther to the east became the crossroads for trade routes reaching thousands of miles north across the Sahara, east toward Egypt, and south toward the Guinea coast. These towns exacted heavy taxes from merchants passing through. Some towns became extremely wealthy.

To gain control of the trade routes, state rulers had to keep extending their borders by conquering neighboring territories. As new states were added to their original holdings, rulers began to build kingdoms. The larger the kingdom, the more taxes from merchants and tribute, or payments or gifts from smaller states, could be collected.

To hold a kingdom or an empire together, a ruler needed tremendous wealth and a great deal of human energy at his disposal in the form of armed forces and workers. The Africans of the western Sudan not only survived but also prospered, and by the third century A.D. the Soninke kingdom of Ghana had been established. It endured for at least six centuries before it was conquered by new forces from the east. The great kingdom of Ghana was to be followed by even larger, wealthier, and more powerful kingdoms.

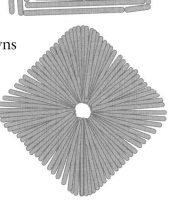

Life in a Kingdom—The Benefits and Drawbacks

We have heard of the glory of the Ghanaian kings and the splendor of their palaces and courts. But what of the ordinary people? What was life in a kingdom like for them? As can be expected when a superpower is imposed on lesser powers, life in a kingdom offered both advantages and disadvantages to ordinary people.

Except for the people in the original state, all others in a kingdom had been conquered. They were forced to pledge allegiance to a foreign ruler who more often than not had a different language and culture from their own. They had to pay tribute. Often, rulers would require certain specialists, such as ironworkers or fishermen, to supply goods to the royal household free of charge. At short notice, men could be drafted into the army to fight the king's wars. Women and children could be taken as slaves or concubines. While the kings amassed vast fortunes in gold and other goods, ordinary folk had no share in this immense wealth.

Once a kingdom had become very wealthy, it naturally attracted many enemies, and so it needed large armies to patrol its borders and fight off invaders. When a kingdom fell through war, its farmlands and cities were destroyed and its people captured or made homeless.

On the other hand, the king's army ensured that trade routes, the key to prosperity, were safe from bandits and robbers. In addition, an efficient king with a large army could force many people of different cultures to live side by side in peace for long periods of time—a benefit for everyone. Although people were certainly oppressed, they may have thought this a small price to pay for peace.

Most kingdoms also developed an intricate system of law and justice. There were strict rules for trade and taxation, and for people's behavior toward one another. These rules ensured that people could live in a law-abiding society.

The Sudanese kingdoms also promoted wide systems of trade.

Most stories of the West African kingdoms are stories of men—kings, warriors, and sorcerers. In some cases, women played powerful political roles as queen mothers or important wives. At the age of 12, boys were circumcised and sent off to learn the traditional craft of their uncle's caste. Wealthier boys went to the cities to study at the universities. Some became apprentices under master craftsmen. At puberty, girls were considered ready to marry. They were forbidden to study, teach, learn crafts, or join the army.

◀ This procession in the modern nation of Niger recalls the ancient kingdoms of the western Sudan. The rich robes and ornate headpieces worn by the horsemen hark back to the prosperous days of the past, as do the horses themselves. Horses imported from North Africa carried soldiers into battle, helping the kings to build their empires.

Through these trade networks many people were kept busy producing things to sell. A common unit of currency also was created for use throughout these and other regions. This currency was the cowrie shell, which was imported from the Indian Ocean. While gold, salt, copper, or cotton cloth were used in some places, it was the cowrie that provided a standard across many frontiers. The cowrie was eventually replaced by the gold dinar. A standard currency created a kind of "common market," which benefited everyone.

Early Contact with the Outside World

North of the Sahara, there had always been close contact among the peoples of North Africa, the Middle East, and the Mediterranean. People, goods, and ideas flowed back and forth along ancient routes. Whatever happened in the north, however, had a distant echo far to the south, in the Sudan.

In 814 B.C., the city of Carthage was founded on the North

▲ African currency took many forms. Cowrie shells, which were imported from the Indian Ocean, were the standard currency for a time in the trade network of the Sudanese kingdoms and in many other areas of Africa.

African coast. Its founders were Phoenicians (foh NEE shuns), who lived at the eastern end of the Mediterranean Sea. Carthage dominated the trade of the western Mediterranean and of West Africa. To this great port came ships from Britain, Spain, Gaul (France), Corsica, Sicily, and Sardinia. Berber merchants traveled south from Carthage, carrying goods to the Sudan on donkeys and in horse-drawn carts. Although the Sahara then was smaller and moister than it later became, to cross it was still a perilous journey.

The Carthaginians themselves rarely penetrated the south and left no traces of any presence in the Sudan. The Berber and Tuareg traders acted as middlemen between the north and the western Sudan, profiting from the lucrative trade that they controlled. It was they who gathered wares for sale and organized the huge camel caravans, sometimes numbering up to

12,000 beasts, that headed south. It was they who had agents all over the western Sudan, and they alone could calculate the real value of a slave, a load of salt, a bundle of hides, or a precious cargo of gold.

Although most of the Berbers' trade was concentrated on routes heading south to the Sudan, they also developed vital links between the western Sudan and regions to the east. One main route bisected the Sahara from Timbuktu to the Nile and went from there to the ports of the Red Sea and the Indian Ocean.

While the Berbers were expanding their trade routes, the Romans were expanding their empire and wanted to control the entire Mediterranean. In 146 B.C., after three long and bloody years of war, the Romans conquered and burned Carthage. But though they had destroyed the city, they had no intention of destroying trade. For the next five centuries, the Romans controlled Carthage's old territories, and the lively trade with West Africa continued.

Many goods from Europe traveled south, and African wares went north.

The Romans also brought Christianity to North Africa. They found converts even among the Berbers, and Christian missionaries spread southeast to Egypt and Ethiopia. But by now the Sahara had become the brutal desert it is today. Travel across it could be achieved only by camels.

In previous millennia, the green and verdant Sahara had perhaps been an inviting place to visit. Now it proved an effective barrier between the north and the south. People on either side of the great desert developed very different cultures and beliefs. Communications became more difficult.

Thus, although Christianity was popular in North Africa for a while, it had no effect on the western Sudan. In any case it hardly had time to gain a foothold in the north before it was swept aside by a new and powerful religion that would greatly influence the course of African history and, in particular, the history of the western Sudan. The new religion was Islam.

MOHAMMED ISLAM

Islam—New Influences in West Africa

Fourteen hundred years ago, most people knew very little about Arabia. It was a distant, barren peninsula dangling between the great African continent to the west and the mass of Asia to the east. There were few towns of importance, and the desert was inhabited mostly by wandering Bedouin tribes and their herds of camels and goats.

Yet in Arabia, in the town of Mecca near the Red Sea, a boy was born in A.D. 570 whose ideas would change the course of world history. His name: Mohammed ibn Abdallah. His idea: Islam.

Ancient Mecca

When Mohammed was born, the town of Mecca was an important trading center. It lay in a dry, rocky valley, surrounded by barren hills and desert. The land was harsh, but Mecca lay at a crossroads for trade routes from the eastern Mediterranean via the Red Sea to the Indian Ocean. Merchants bringing goods from Ethiopia, China, India, Egypt, and Europe came to Mecca to bargain in the bazaars. Then they traveled west over the harshest desert in the world to trade in the Sudan and returned laden with the riches of Ghana and other kingdoms.

Along these age-old trade routes came pilgrims as well as goods, for Mecca was the site of the Kaaba (KAH bah), an ancient and very holy shrine that contained a sacred stone. Arabs came from hundreds of miles away to worship the stone and other idols by walking around the Kaaba seven times. They believed the stone had fallen from the sky and was a link with the High God, Allah, and other deities.

In the deserts of Arabia at that time, Bedouin tribes lived in fierce competition with one another for the basic necessities of life. Tribes near Mecca had begun to profit from the great fortunes to be made in the city. In the old nomadic days, desert clans had depended on one another to survive. Now, as families and individuals became wealthier, ancient tribal codes were breaking down. Family disputes turned into bloody feuds that only death could end, and rivals were said to tear out the hearts of their conquered enemies. These tribes kept the Arabian sands in a constant state of war and turmoil, ruled not by law but by the sword.

This was the land into which Mohammed was born.

Islam Is Born

Mohammed grew up to be an extremely devout man. He wished to find some way of bringing peace to his country and returning to the values that had traditionally helped people to survive.

Each year Mohammed made a spiritual retreat to Mount Hira, just outside Mecca. According to Islamic belief, Mohammed was possessed by an extraordinary vision during one such retreat. He saw the archangel Gabriel, who handed him a written scroll. Amazingly, although he could neither read nor write, Mohammed was able to read it.

The legend tells how the scroll ordered Mohammed to preach that there is only one God, Allah—the all-powerful, the all-merciful. The angel Gabriel also warned Mohammed against the worship of idols like the statues in the Kaaba. In this way, Muslims believe, Mohammed received the word of the Lord and became the Lord's prophet.

Flight from Mecca

In A.D. 610, at the age of 40, Mohammed began to preach the religion of Islam in the city of Mecca. The Arab word *Islam* means "submission," and Muslims are those who submit to the one God, Allah.

Although Mohammed won over a few important converts, he was scorned by many citizens of Mecca, while others plotted to kill him. When some pilgrims invited him to preach in the northern city of Medina, he decided to move there. In A.D. 622, Mohammed quietly left Mecca one night with a single companion and made his way north. This journey—the Hegira (hih JEE ruh) or Flight—marks the first year of the Islamic calendar, the year A.H. 1.

The Gathering Forces

In Medina the further teachings of Islam came to Mohammed over a period of time as a series of revelations. Since he could not write, he memorized them and preached them to his followers, who wrote them down in Arabic. These teachings included matters of belief and also dictated the proper manners, customs, education, eating habits, and marital relations of good Muslims. Called verses, or *sura* (SOO ruh), they were

Islam, Christianity, and Judaism

Mecca was a crossroads where many people of different beliefs came together. Mohammed was familiar with both Judaism and Christianity, which were well established long before he was born. Some of the stories in the Quran are similar to those in the Bible, the holy book of the Christians, and in the Torah (TOH ruh), the holy book of the Jews. Like Jews and Christians, Muslims believe in one God. Allah, they say, created the world in six days and allowed Adam, the first man, to live in Paradise until Satan tempted him into sin. The followers of Islam believe that life on earth is preparation for eternal life in Paradise. Angels record a

eventually collected into one book, the Quran, the holy book of Islam.

By A.D. 630, only eight years after the Hegira, Mohammed had succeeded in uniting many of the pagan factions of Arabia into a formidable army under the banner of Islam. That year, he returned to Mecca as the leader of a triumphant Islamic force. The city surrendered with little bloodshed, and Mohammed destroyed the idols in the Kaaba. Most Meccans became Muslims, and person's deeds in life and decide on Judgment Day whether that person will go to Paradise or Hell. The Quran describes Paradise as a place in which there are "gardens of dark green" with luscious fruit, "gushing fountains," and "plentiful meat"—all things that people in the hot, barren lands of Arabia must often have longed for.

Muslims also believe that Mary gave birth to Jesus, but, like the Jews, they do not recognize Jesus as the son of God. Instead, Muslims see Jesus as one of a great line of prophets that includes Moses, Noah, and Abraham. Mohammed, they say, was the last and the greatest of the prophets.

a mosque was built around the shrine. Mohammed made some ancient rituals, such as the circling of the Kaaba seven times, part of the Muslim pilgrim's ritual. Mecca and Medina became the holy cities of Islam, which they have remained to this day.

The Islamic Faith

Mohammed did not live to see Islam become a conquering force in the world. He died in A.D. 632. But he left behind a faith that within a hun-

dred years had united millions of people in an empire stretching from West Africa to India. Today, about 1 billion people all over the world are Muslims, and Islam has lost none of the energy with which it was founded over a thousand years ago.

Muslims worship in special temples called mosques where prayers are led by a devout Muslim called an *imam*. Praying at the mosque is especially important on Fridays, the Muslims' sacred day. (Sunday is sacred for Christians, and Saturday for Jews.) The times for prayer are announced by a *muezzin* (moo EZ ihn), an official who calls from a minaret, or tall tower, near the mosque. Wherever they happen to be—at home, at work, or even in the street—Muslims always pray facing Mecca.

Islam Moves out of Arabia

Mohammed wanted to spread his teachings farther afield but died before he could do so. His followers, however, were men from the cruel Arabian desert who were eager to find better lands. In the name of the holy war, or *jihad*, they were also ready to bring the word of Allah to the nonbe-

The Great Mosque in Mopti, a town on the Niger River in Mali, is made of mud. Each year thousands of citizens gather to repair its walls after the rainy season. Because they were also made of mud, most of the palaces and even some whole cities described by early travelers have disappeared.

lievers of the world. If they died fighting for Islam, they would reap the rewards of Paradise that the Quran promised. And so they began to move out of the Arabian peninsula.

Only ten years after Mohammed's death, the Muslims had conquered Syria, Palestine, and Egypt. Later, they also conquered Iraq, Persia (Iran), and Afghanistan. Muslims also traveled down the Red Sea into the Indian Ocean and along the east coast of Africa. They carried Islam with them to the great trading ports on the coasts of present-day Somalia, Kenya, and Tanzania.

In North Africa, Muslims met heavy resistance from the Berbers. But by A.D. 661, Islam had replaced Christianity in North Africa, which became and has remained deeply Muslim in its culture and legal system. It was Islamic Berber merchants who carried their faith south over the caravan routes to Ghana and the western Sudan.

Islam in Africa

The early Muslims conquered vast territories in their zeal to gain new converts to Islam. They were followed by

●●●●●●●●●●

When people become Muslims, they declare their faith in a statement known as the *shahada:* "There is no God but Allah and Mohammed is His Prophet."

The Five Pillars of Islam are the rules that every good Muslim must follow.

● Muslims must believe in Allah as the one and only God.

● Muslims must pray five times a day, facing toward Mecca.

● Muslims must give alms to the poor.

● Muslims must fast from sunrise to sunset each day of Ramadan, the ninth month in the Islamic year.

● Muslims must make a *hajj* (hahj), or pilgrimage, to Mecca at least once in their lifetime if they can afford to do so.

more peaceful merchants and teachers who wanted to spread the faith.

There were several reasons why foreign lands adopted Islam quickly. In the early days, people were simply forced to convert—or die. Later, Islam was relatively tolerant of other religions. Conquered peoples were neither killed nor enslaved. In fact, the Quran encouraged Muslims to free slaves. The Islamic governors, or caliphs, however, imposed heavy taxes on those who refused to convert. This gave many nonbelievers a good reason to accept the faith, if only superficially. And once nonbelievers had converted to Islam, they were accepted by their conquerors as equals.

Early Muslims in Africa quickly developed their own communities by establishing mosques, complete with the distinctive minaret for calling the prayers. Mosques also functioned as schools, courts, and centers for religious ceremonies and festivals.

All Muslims, including children, were required to learn the entire Quran by heart, as they still do today. Because the Quran was written in Arabic, literacy in the language spread rapidly. Africans who could speak and write Arabic were able to communicate with other Arabic-speaking peoples from the Atlantic to the Red Sea and beyond. The ability to speak Arabic was a great advantage in trade, and Arabic soon became the *lingua franca,* or international language, for the exchange of ideas and information. For the merchant princes of Gao (GAH oh), Timbuktu, and other cities, Islam offered membership in a highly privi-

leged, international trading club. Their journeys to Mecca put them in touch with merchants from Egypt, Arabia, and Asia and vastly increased the import/export market.

With the Arabic language came Arab learning, which profoundly impressed and influenced Africans. Since Islam had spread far and wide, its culture blended art, architecture, and music from Egypt, Arabia, Persia, India, other parts of Asia, and

Muslim children learn the Quran. Many devout Muslims still commit the holy book to memory — an amazing feat, considering that the Quran contains nearly 80,000 words. ▼

Europe. Arab Muslims brought with them centuries-old knowledge in literature, geography, history, mathematics, astronomy, and other areas of science, especially medicine. African scholars eager for the new learning could attend the great universities established by the Muslims. Those in Timbuktu and Jenne (JE ne) on the Niger River became world-famous and attracted scholars from as far away as Spain and Libya.

The rulers of early kingdoms in the western Sudan were anxious to attract Muslim trade from the north. They therefore welcomed Muslims and seemed willing to accept Islam. The kings of Ghana, as you will remember, even allowed Muslims their own trading town at Kumbi. But they were placed in an awkward position because the people they ruled still clung to their old beliefs, and the kings needed their loyalty as well as Muslim business. Thus, playing the coin on both sides, these early kings tended to convert outwardly to Islam while still practicing their native religions among their own people. By the thirteenth century, however, the rulers of several kingdoms in the western Sudan had

become true believers in Islam. Some of them even undertook the *hajj,* or pilgrimage, to Mecca, thousands of miles to the east.

The arrival of Islam was a double-edged sword for the western Sudan. On the one hand, trade prospered and opened up contact to the outside world. On the other, tensions between African Muslim leaders and their non-Muslim subjects often caused serious tribal division and could shake a kingdom to its foundations. In Ghana, the Muslim Almoravids were able to find Islamic supporters who helped them overthrow the king. The Almoravid invasion eventually led to the tragic downfall of the kingdom.

From the start, Islam in West Africa tended to be the religion of the kings and chiefs, who had strong political motives for converting. The common folk in the rural areas, on the other hand, continued as they always had. Thus for centuries Islam did not replace traditional beliefs but thrived alongside them. Islam, along with Christianity, is still a major religion in West Africa today.

▲ Muslims bow in prayer at a Mosque.

لا إله إلا الله محمد رسول الله

4

Mali—The Mandinka Empire

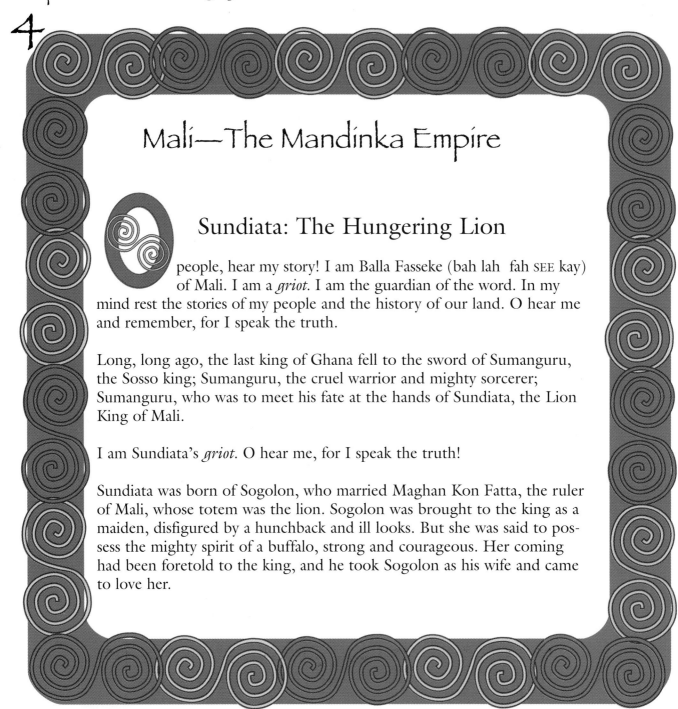

Sundiata: The Hungering Lion

people, hear my story! I am Balla Fasseke (bah lah fah SEE kay) of Mali. I am a *griot*. I am the guardian of the word. In my mind rest the stories of my people and the history of our land. O hear me and remember, for I speak the truth.

Long, long ago, the last king of Ghana fell to the sword of Sumanguru, the Sosso king; Sumanguru, the cruel warrior and mighty sorcerer; Sumanguru, who was to meet his fate at the hands of Sundiata, the Lion King of Mali.

I am Sundiata's *griot*. O hear me, for I speak the truth!

Sundiata was born of Sogolon, who married Maghan Kon Fatta, the ruler of Mali, whose totem was the lion. Sogolon was brought to the king as a maiden, disfigured by a hunchback and ill looks. But she was said to possess the mighty spirit of a buffalo, strong and courageous. Her coming had been foretold to the king, and he took Sogolon as his wife and came to love her.

When Sundiata was born, the king rejoiced. The great royal drums carried the news all over the kingdom. But his first wife, Sassouma, was jealous. Her son should inherit the throne! What need had her husband of another son? She vowed that Sundiata would never become king.

In time, Sassouma saw that she had nothing to fear, for Sundiata was stricken by a strange infirmity. He could neither speak nor walk! How great was Sogolon's sorrow! For seven long years, she tried to cure her son. She consulted with all the wise men of the kingdom and brewed herbs and potions, but to no avail. And Sundiata's father, King Maghan Kon Fatta, despaired. But his *griot,* who was my father, advised the king. "The young seed must endure the storm," he said. "And from this small seed shall spring a great tree."

One day, when the king felt death approach, he called the child to him. "I shall give you the gift each king gives to his heir," he said. And on that day, my people, the king gave me—Balla Fasseke—to Sundiata to be his *griot,* as my father had been the king's *griot,* and his father before that. And on that day, for the first time in his life, Sundiata spoke. "Balla, you shall be my *griot,*" he said. And the king knew that his son—the son of the lion and the buffalo—was worthy to be king.

But when Maghan Kon Fatta died, the councilors ignored his wishes. It was the son of Sassouma who ascended the throne, and not Sundiata, the rightful heir. And Sassouma persecuted Sogolon and her son with evil hatred and banished them to a dark corner of the palace. Oh, how Sogolon's tears flowed in her unhappiness! When Sundiata saw his mother's despair, he looked at her calmly and said, "Today I will walk." Then he sent me, Balla Fasseke, to the royal forges. "Tell the smiths to make me the sturdiest iron rod possible," he ordered.

Six men were needed to carry the iron rod to Sogolon's house. They threw it on the ground before Sundiata. A huge multitude of people had gathered to

see if Sundiata would walk. "Arise, young lion!" I commanded. "Roar, and may the land know that from henceforth, it has a master!"

Sundiata gripped the rod with his two hands and held it upright in the ground. Beads of sweat poured from his face. A deathly silence gripped the people. All at once, with a mighty thrust, Sundiata stood upright. The crowd gasped. The iron rod was bent like a bow. And Sogolon, who had been dumb with amazement, suddenly burst into song:

> Oh day, oh beautiful day,
> Oh day, day of joy,
> Allah Almighty, this is the finest
> day you have created,
> My son is going to walk!
> Hear me, people, for I speak the truth!

Sundiata threw away the rod, and his first steps were those of a giant.

From that day on, Sundiata grew in strength. He became a fine hunter and was much loved by all the people. But Sassouma, whose son was now king, feared Sundiata's growing power. Her plots to kill him failed. And she knew that I would perform any deed to bring Sundiata to the throne. So, to separate us, Sassouma sent me far away to the court of the demon king, Sumanguru. And there I remained for several years. I pretended allegiance to Sumanguru, but always I waited for the day when I would sing the praises of Sundiata once more.

Sogolon fled the palace and took Sundiata far from Sassouma's hatred. For seven years they lived in exile, finding food and shelter wherever they could. At last, they came to

the city of Mema. Here they met with good luck, for the king of Mema took a liking to Sundiata and treated him like a son. He admired Sundiata's courage and leadership. This king decided to make the young boy his heir and teach him the arts of government and war. And thus, Sundiata grew to manhood.

One day, messengers came running to Sundiata. "Sumanguru has invaded Mali!" they cried. "The king and his mother, Sassouma, have fled. Only you can save our people. Return, young lion, and reclaim your throne!"

This, O people, was the moment of Sundiata's destiny. The king of Mema gave him half his forces. And as Sundiata rode at their head, more and more men joined him until a great army thundered across the plains. And from far-distant Mali, Sumanguru, too, raced to meet his destiny. And I, O my people, I followed, for I knew that soon I would be reunited with Sundiata, my Lion King.

And so it was. Sundiata led his army from Mema, and Sumanguru came from Mali. The two great armies met in battle on the plains of Kirina. I took my chance and escaped at last from Sumanguru. Through the thick

The soldiers who rode into battle with Sundiata at Kirina may have resembled the horseman represented in this fourteenth century Malian sculpture.

clouds of dust and the battle cries of the warriors, I galloped to Sundiata's side. Oh, how great was our joy!

My years with Sumanguru had not been in vain, O my people, for I had learned that Sumanguru feared the magic power of a white rooster. He believed that one touch of the rooster's spur would defeat him forever. And this very spur I had fastened to an arrow, which I gave to my lord, Sundiata.

With deadly aim, Sundiata sent the arrow speeding across the battlefield toward Sumanguru. True as a hawk in flight, it met its mark, grazing the sorcerer's shoulder. With a great scream of fear, Sumanguru turned on his horse and fled.

Far away he rode, to the caves of Mount Koulikoro. There we saw Sumanguru, the demon king, fall to his knees and turn to stone. His soldiers, discouraged by his flight, ceased to fight and were defeated.

And so Sundiata returned to Mali to reclaim his throne, and I, Balla Fasseke, went with him to sing of his glory. There waited the twelve kings who had helped Sundiata in exile. Each thrust his great lance into the earth before Sundiata. "We shall be united!" they proclaimed. "You have restored peace to our lands. We give you our kingdoms to rule in your great wisdom!" The drums beat out the news. The warriors danced in a joyous frenzy. And the crowd sent a mighty cry to the heavens: "Wassa, Wassa, Ayé (WAH sah EYE ay)!"*

And thus did I bear witness to the birth of the great kingdom of Mali. And thus did I see Sundiata become its first emperor.

So listen, O my people, and remember, for I speak the truth. May you live to tell this story to your children, that the name of Sundiata—the Lion King— shall live forever.

*A Mandinka cry of joy

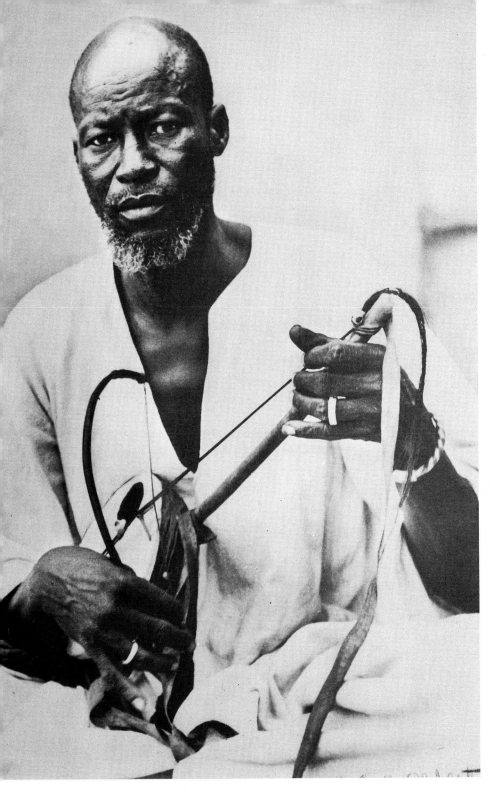

Sundiata Conquers the Sosso

To this day, the story of Sundiata, the Hungering Lion, is told by West African griots. The details often vary, but much of the story has been confirmed as fact by historians.

Sumanguru was the king of Sosso who conquered Ghana. The neighboring kingdom of Kangaba (kan GAH bah), which was located on the Niger River about 400 km (250 mi) south of Kumbi, was one of the smaller states that had broken away from Ghana. Now the Mandinka people of this area were expanding their own kingdom and presented a serious threat to Sumanguru's power.

In one fell swoop Sumanguru annexed Kangaba and had the eleven brothers who were the heirs to the throne of Kangaba assassinated. For some reason,

◀ A present-day *griot* plays an instrument called a *kora* as accompaniment to his ballads. He keeps alive the ancient as well as the more recent histories of his people.

however, he did not kill the twelfth heir, Sundiata. Perhaps he took pity on him because he could not walk. More probably, he believed that Sundiata presented no threat to his own power.

The Mandinka people believed that it was Sundiata's very name—the Hungering Lion—that gave the young prince the strength and determination to walk and later to rule. Sundiata became an expert hunter and horseman. During his exile from Kangaba, he developed a reputation for courage and military skill among the rulers of neighboring states. It was these rulers who united and came to his aid when Sumanguru invaded Mali. By 1230, Sundiata had been proclaimed king of Mali. The great battle between the Mali and Sosso forces took place in 1235.

After his defeat at Kirina, Sumanguru disappeared from history. Sundiata, meanwhile, went on to conquer the enemy capital at Sosso and other important Sosso cities. Sundiata now moved his capital south to Niani (NEE ah nee), the city of his birth.

And from there, he proceeded to build a central government that would establish peace and order throughout the kingdom.

The Niger Helps a Kingdom Grow

The kingdom of Ghana developed around the city of Kumbi, at a small oasis on a trade route between North Africa and the gold-bearing lands to the south. Mali, on the other hand, developed around its capital of Niani, on the Niger River. The river stretched from the southern borders of the kingdom for hundreds of miles to its eastern boundary. Whereas the people of Ghana had only camels and donkeys for transport, the Malians had the river as well as animals. They could transport bulk goods and large loads much faster and more easily by river than by land.

The people who lived on the fertile lands near the Niger suffered less from drought or lack of rainfall than those living in the drier regions to the north. In these flat areas by the river, food was grown not only for local people but for those living in cities farther up the Niger and in oasis towns along trade routes to the north.

The Mandinka word *mali* means "where the king lives" and eventually became the name of the empire. The southern part of the modern nation of Mali lies within the borders of the ancient kingdom.

▲ The Niger River is the main thoroughfare of the western Sudan. On its banks, farmers, nomads, fishermen, and villagers meet at a thriving marketplace.

The Niger thus enabled the kingdom of Mali to develop a far more stable economy than Ghana had had, and contributed to the rise of the Malian empire, which was far more extensive than the kingdom of Ghana. The Niger also was a key factor in both Timbuktu's emergence as a city of international renown and the development of trade between the western Sudan, North Africa, and lands to the east.

When Sundiata returned to Niani from a political tour or a hunting trip, he was greeted by this song:

•

He has come,
And happiness has
come.
Sundiata is here
And happiness is here.

•

Sundiata Sets the Stage

Sumanguru's 33 years of rule in Ghana had brought trade to a standstill, and years of war had left the territories of Mali in turmoil. It was up to Sundiata to restore order.

Mali now encompassed a vast area three times the size of Ghana. It included the goldfields of Bambuk and Bure and the great cities of Timbuktu and Gao on the Niger and was close to the salt mines of Taghaza. The seat of government was at Niani, but Sundiata also appointed governors for the outer states. The farthest kingdoms were ruled by their former kings, who pledged allegiance to Mali. They reinforced their loyalty with tribute—annual gifts of rice, millet, arrows, and lances.

To maintain the empire's power, an adequate food supply for the people was needed. Because there was no major war to fight, soldiers and captured slaves could now work as farmers. With marvelous foresight, Sundiata had new farmlands cleared and planted with peanuts, beans, rice, onions, sorghum, papaya, calabashes, and other crops. From the east, he also introduced cotton, which was to become a valuable commodity. His soldiers learned to breed and care for cattle, sheep, goats, and poultry. Under Sundiata's leadership, Mali became one of the richest farming regions in West Africa.

Sundiata was a devout Muslim. His faith enabled him to quickly reestablish commercial relations with the Muslim merchants who had stopped trading with Ghana when the kingdom was conquered by Sumanguru. The merchants had established a new trading center at Walata, to the northeast of Kumbi. From there, trade routes had been set up once again to the salt mines of the north and the gold mines of the south.

Sundiata was indeed a great leader. He unified many different peoples in a true federation of states. He was a visionary who laid the foundations for one of the greatest empires Africa has known. Sadly, Sundiata did not live to see the fruits of his wisdom. Some say he was killed by accident in a riding tournament. Others say he drowned. His name, however, lives on to this day in the songs, poems, and dances of the western Sudan.

The Golden Age of Mali

Mansa Musa: The Black Moses of Mali

It was the year 1324. Mansa Musa (MAHN suh MOO suh), the king of Mali, rode across the desert in grand style. He wore a fine turban of many lengths of cotton wound around his head. His marvelous robes of embroidered silk flowed with the wind. The king's camel was decked in colorful padded cloths, with a saddle of the finest red leather. Near the king rode the royal guard, their shields and lances flashing in the sun. With them were the standard bearers, who carried the banners of the kingdom across the desert sands.

A devout Muslim, Musa was making his pilgrimage to the holy shrine at Mecca, 4,800 km (3,000 mi) to the east. But it was also said that Musa had accidentally killed his own mother. In his agony and remorse, he wished to abdicate the throne to his son. The rest of his days, he swore, would be spent in fasting and prayer at Mecca. With this pilgrimage, Musa hoped to find peace in his heart.

With Mansa Musa rode many escorts. Some say they numbered 60,000! His senior wife, Inari-Kunate (ee NAH ree koo NAH tay), and her 500 maids and slaves traveled with him. Soldiers, relatives, friends, teachers, and doctors joined the great king on his pilgrimage. The chiefs and princes of all the states of the empire were also present, splendidly clad in their royal robes. They were accompanied by their own soldiers, families, and servants. Each night, when camp was made, the royal *griots* and musicians composed their lovely, lilting ballads to commemorate the glorious event for history.

In Niani, preparations for the journey had occupied the court for months. The king's officers had to outfit the huge entourage for a year or longer, and no expense was spared. Provisions piled up in the royal storerooms, and hundreds of horses, camels, cattle, and goats for the journey roamed the pastures.

A call went out to all corners of the kingdom for gold, gold, and more gold. A hundred camel loads of gold were prepared, each weighing 135 kg (300 lb). Five hundred slaves were to march with the king. For each, a staff of solid gold was fashioned.

The palace diviners had set the most auspicious, or lucky, date for departure. It was to be a Saturday, falling on the twelfth day of the month. The king had waited nine long months for just such a day. When it came, the royal drums beat out the signal for departure, and the tremendous caravan set forth.

From Niani, the king traveled along the Niger to Timbuktu and then north across the Sahara toward the salt mines of Taghaza. In the searing heat of day and the freezing cold of the desert nights, the caravan journeyed from one oasis to another. Slowly they inched across the barren wastelands, ever eastward toward Egypt and then southward along the Arabian shore of the Red Sea to Mecca.

Long before Mansa Musa's glittering caravan arrived in Cairo, the news of his coming had spread, for he was the richest and most powerful of the African Muslim kings. He was far richer than the rulers of Egypt and governed an empire almost as large as Europe. He was a king greatly feared by his enemies but also greatly respected for his wisdom and generosity.

The emir of Cairo welcomed Mansa Musa in the name of the glorious sultan el Malik en Nasir (el mah LEEK en NAH sur). Although the great king spoke perfect Arabic, he wished to demonstrate his power and thus spoke to the emir only through an interpreter. Musa was required by royal protocol to visit the sultan at his palace. But he refused, declaring that he could not confuse his pilgrimage to Mecca with any other business. In truth, Mansa was reluctant to kiss the ground before the sultan, or to kiss his hand, as was required. After all, he, Mansa Musa of Mali, was the most powerful ruler of the Sudan, before whom his subjects bowed to the ground and poured dust on their heads!

Eventually the king agreed to visit the sultan. But privately, Musa declared that when he bowed to the ground, it would be to honor Allah, not el Malik en Nasir.

The sultan greeted Mansa Musa with all the pomp and ceremony due such a great king. He housed the royal entourage in a fine palace and gave the visitors ceremonial robes of honor. He entertained them with feasts and dances. When October came and it was time for Mansa Musa to leave, the sultan showered him with drachmas (DRAK mahs), or silver coins, and presented him with many choice camels, complete with saddles and harnesses. He stocked the caravan with provisions and established feeding stations for the animals along the entire route to Mecca.

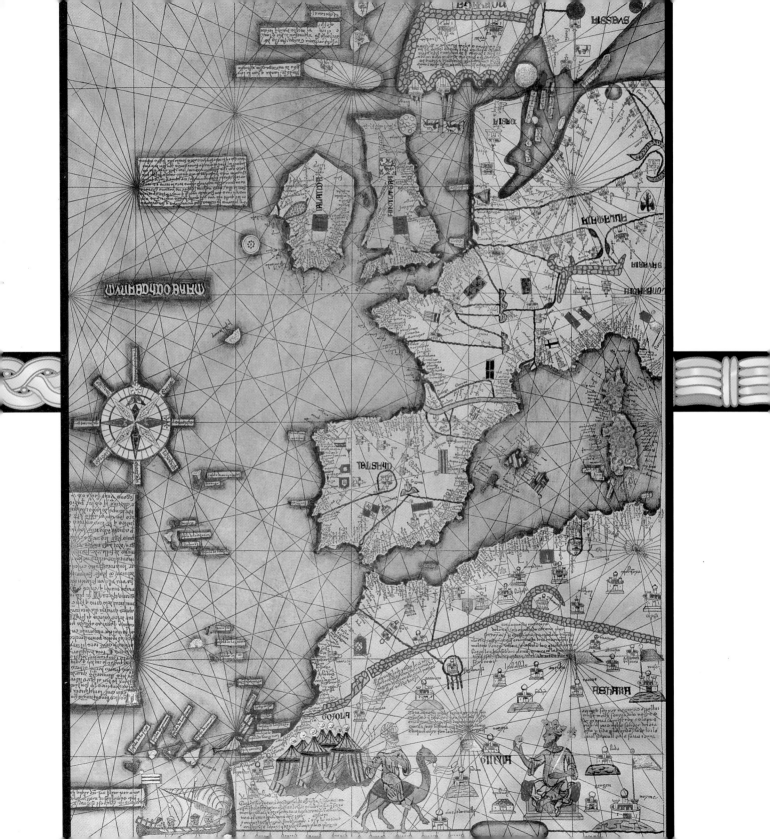

Such was the generosity of the Egyptian sultan! But it appeared as nothing compared with the generosity of Mansa Musa himself. In Mecca and Medina, he distributed abundant alms and presents to the people. On his return to Cairo, he gave every single officer of the court a large sum of gold. The good emir himself received thousands of ingots of raw gold. And happy were the Egyptian merchants, who made huge profits from Musa's pilgrimage!

When Mansa Musa left Egypt to return home, his fame had spread throughout Europe, Asia, and Egypt. He was indeed the *khan* (king) of Africa! The mighty kingdom of Mali became known as the land of limitless gold. And many were those who journeyed there to see for themselves the greatness of King Musa and the glory of his empire.

The Golden Age of Mali

Mansa Musa was a grandson of one of Sundiata's sisters. He ruled Mali for 25 years, and his many achievements have been well recorded in both oral and written histories of the time.

After Sundiata's death in 1255, the rulers of Mali took the title *Mansa*, which means "emperor" or "sultan." Sundiata's son Mansa Wali was the first Malian king to make the pilgrimage to Mecca, establishing a long Muslim tradition.

During the years that followed Sundiata's death, various leaders struggled for power. Just as the kingdom seemed on the verge of collapse, Mansa Musa took the throne. The name *Musa* means "Moses," and he is often referred to in history as "the black Moses."

◀ In this map of 1375, Mansa Musa of Mali holds a gold nugget out to an Arab trader approaching on camelback. Mansa Musa's pilgrimage to Mecca helped to spread the news of Mali's wealth far and wide and attracted many to Musa's court and the kingdom's markets.

"Mansa Musa holds court in his palace on a great balcony called a *bembe* (bem be) where he has a great seat of ebony that is like a throne . . . On either side it is flanked by elephant tusks. His arms [weapons] stand near him, being all of gold—saber, lance, quiver, bow and arrows. He wears wide trousers made of about twenty pieces of material which he alone may wear. Behind him there stand a score or so of Turkish pages bought for him in Cairo. One of them, at his left, holds a silk umbrella . . ."

—Al Omari, Egyptian historian, 1325

The Glorious *Hajj*

Mansa Musa's pilgrimage to Mecca was the sensation of the Muslim world. It was, in fact, one of the most famous trips in all history! The remarkable event was chronicled by Muslim, Jewish, and Christian historians.

During his *hajj*, Mansa Musa was so generous with his gold that he embarrassed himself and his court by running out of money. The king was forced to borrow funds for the return journey from Egyptian merchants. They gladly lent the money—at a high interest rate, of course—knowing that the king of Mali could be trusted to pay back his debt. Meanwhile, however, Musa had put so much gold into circulation that its value on the Cairo market fell sharply. It was 12 years or more before the gold market recovered.

Musa proved himself an exceptionally wise ruler. He took many heads of state and young princes with him on the pilgrimage. Some had to go as hostages to ensure that they would not start any rebellions, and that Musa's son could rule in peace while the king was absent. Only a king as powerful as Musa could dare leave his empire for almost a year without fear of losing the throne.

On his way home from Mecca, Mansa Musa's generals gave him a welcome-home gift. They had captured Gao, capital city of the Songhay kingdom, some 800 km (500 mi) to the northeast. To ensure the city's loyalty, Musa took two Songhay princes with him as hostages, a move that would later prove fatal to the kingdom of Mali.

Whether Mansa Musa had really killed his own mother or not remains the stuff of legend. He never realized his dream of handing the kingdom over to his son and returning to Mecca for the rest of his life. One thing or another kept Musa at home until his death in 1337.

Good Government—A Long Tradition

Like Sundiata and some of the great kings of Ghana, Mansa Musa was an extremely efficient ruler. His greatest challenge as emperor was to bring peace to the ravaged kingdom. From the capital at Niani, Musa personally appointed his staff and kept a sharp watch for any signs of trouble. The central part of the empire was divided into provinces, each with its own governor, or *ferba*. There were several important towns in the empire, each administered by a *mochrif* (moh KREEF), or mayor. Many regions of the Malian empire remained partly independent, but their rulers had to pay allegiance to the king.

There were often rebellions in the smaller kingdoms bordering the central part of the empire. Like the rulers of ancient Ghana, Mansa Musa maintained a huge army to keep the peace. These soldiers also policed the many trade routes, keeping them safe for merchants from the north, south, and east. Writing in the later part of Musa's reign, the globe-trotting historian Ibn Battuta, who traveled through Mali, commented: "There is complete security in their country. Neither traveler nor inhabitant in it has anything to fear from robbers or men of violence."

The army pushed the borders of the kingdom ever outward. It carried the banners of Mali from the Atlantic coast in the west beyond the cities of Timbuktu and Gao in the east; from

The legendary city of Timbuktu was a center of learning, luxury, and trade located on the great bend of the Niger River. Here, river people met with the desert nomads, and Timbuktu developed from a tent settlement to a sprawling city. Timbuktu's main attractions were its universities, stone palace, and bustling markets. It was home to the very rich and the very poor, to scholars and merchants from Africa, the Middle East, and even Europe. ▼

According to legend, Abubakar gave up the throne to his brother, Mansa Musa, and moved to the plains near the Atlantic Ocean. There he assembled a vast army of craftsmen to build a fleet of ships. When all was ready, Abubakar, dressed in a long white robe and jeweled turban, left Mali. He sailed down the River Senegal and out into the Atlantic.

Abubakar may have reached the Americas, following much the same currents as Columbus more than a century later. He may have used Arab sailors, who were skilled at navigating both the desert, a "sea of sand," and the Indian Ocean, which they regularly crossed.

the salt mines of Taghaza in the north to the fabled gold mines of Wangara in the south. The Egyptian historian Al Omari, who lived at the same time as Mansa Musa, wrote that Mali was "square in shape, being four months [of travel] in length and at least as much in breadth"—perhaps 2,400 km by 1,600 km (1,500 mi by 1,000 mi).

Security and prosperity may have led Mali to seek fortunes even farther afield. Mansa Musa's brother Abubakar (ah-boo BAH kahr) is said to have equipped an armada of several hundred ships. Twice he set off across the Atlantic in search of land. His was the only ship to survive the first journey. There were no survivors of the second voyage.

As the empire grew in size, it became increasingly difficult to control. Each of the many different states in Mali had its own leader. By tradition, the king could claim allegiance only from leaders who recognized him as *their* king, descended from a related royal family. This kinship system limited the loyalty the king could expect. Mansa Musa had other supporters, however. Muslim schools were producing a class of educated, literate men, who could organize

government and trade efficiently. These men were neutral, free from the claims of kinship. They were of great help to Mansa Musa in uniting the empire.

Trade and Finance
The empire of Mali was built on much the same foundation as Ghana, which had developed from a group of small states into a flourishing empire. Sundiata had laid the groundwork for thriving agriculture. The Mandinka people hunted elephant, buffalo, and hippopotamus. They were also skilled at the traditional crafts of iron smelting, wood carving, metal-working, weaving, tanning, and dyeing, all of which had had their roots in Ghana.

But the mainstay of the kingdom's economy was trade, not agriculture. Mali had taken over the old trade routes established in Ghana, and with them the precious gold-salt exchange. The trade routes crisscrossed the Sahara from north to south like the pulsing arteries of a living organism. From Niani, caravans traveled to Sijilmasa, Fez, and Sus (soos), via Gao to the Fezzan (fez AN), and to Ghadames (guh DAM ez). The routes were linked by a network of east-west tributaries. From the north came salt, iron, and copper, cloth, books, pearls, cowrie shells, and other goods. Gold, kola nuts, ivory, leather, rubber, and slaves traveled the age-old paths from the south. The kingdom amassed great wealth from the heavy taxes levied on all goods.

To protect the more westerly routes, Mansa Musa sent ambassadors to establish friendly relations with the sultan of Fez in Morocco. After all, Mali's borders stretched so far north that the two regions were practically neighbors. Nevertheless, there were times during Musa's reign when Berber robbers made these trade

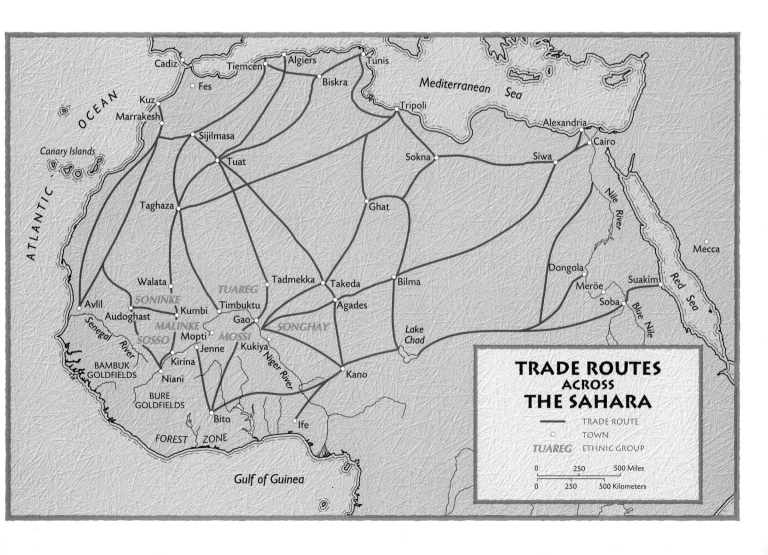

TRADE ROUTES
ACROSS
THE SAHARA

— TRADE ROUTE
○ TOWN
TUAREG ETHNIC GROUP

0   250   500 Miles
0   250   500 Kilometers

routes too risky. In fact, since the Almoravid invasion of Ghana in the eleventh century, merchants had been favoring routes farther to the east. Some of these were efficiently maintained by private businessmen, who provided water wells and guards.

The Berbers ran the Saharan trade routes, and the Mandinke people controlled trade between the grasslands and the coast to the south, and the big Sudanese markets to the north. They efficiently exploited their position as middlemen by organizing themselves into companies. Calling themselves Dyula (dee OO luh), a name that survives to this day, they traveled far and wide over the western Sudan. The Dyula were united as Muslims and helped to spread Islam wherever they went.

Under Mansa Musa, an important new trade route was established. This route took a northeasterly direction across the Sahara to Cairo in Egypt. Many Egyptian traders, scholars, and religious leaders traveled the new route to Mali, forging strong economic and cultural links between the two nations.

In all the kingdoms, artisans such as blacksmiths, weavers, and potters were very important. Their work was considered a gift from God. Each artisan understood the deep symbolic meaning of his craft. In Mali, for example, all 33 parts of a weaver's loom had meaning. Four parts of the frame were symbols of the female elements—earth, air, fire, and water. Four parts symbolized the directions—north, south, east, and west. Before working, a weaver touched each part of his loom and recited a special prayer.

The new route passed through Takedda (tah KAY duh), where copper was mined in huge quantities. Copper bars were exchanged for goods, and the metal was used to make tools, ornaments, utensils, and household objects. Mansa Musa once remarked that copper was his most important source of revenue.

During this time, Mali was the main source of gold for all of Europe and Arabia. The Wangara people still controlled the mines and carried on their secretive silent barter for salt. But new sources of the precious metal had been found to the southeast of the empire. These replaced the exhausted mines at Bambuk and Bure in the west, which had financed the kingdom of Ghana for centuries.

With the new trade route and the new gold mines, the center of power in the western Sudan gradually shifted to the east—and would continue to shift eastward for another 500 years.

Daily Life

For most people in Mali, life went on as it always had. The Tuareg (TAW reg), Wolof (WOH luhf), Malinke (mah LIHN ke), Bambara,

For hundreds of years, West African gold fueled trade between the Sudan, Europe, and the East. The Muslim dinar became the international currency familiar in huge areas of the known world. In the thirteenth century, the Italian cities of Venice, Genoa, and Florence began minting florins and ducats from West African gold. These coins financed the growing trade network of the Europeans. When American gold was found in the fifteenth century, African gold had already helped build Europe into a superpower. African slave labor would help solidify that position for the next five centuries.

Songhay, and Fulbe (FOOL be) peoples of the empire had somewhat different ways of life, but, through force and good government, the king had managed to unite them under his banner.

The empire was remarkably safe, as Ibn Battuta noted. He also reported that Mansa Musa was an extremely just though stern ruler, who brought law and order to the land. The people were notably honest. Battuta reported that if a Berber person died in Mali, the Africans kept all his belongings carefully—sometimes for decades—until the proper heirs could be traced.

The royal household collected untold riches in solid gold, gold dinars, silks, ivory, and other valuable goods. Mansa Musa was generous to his officers and soldiers. He gave them gifts of land, horses, and clothing. The highest officials received up to 400 pounds of gold a year! Even the common people seemed to enjoy a fairly high standard of living, though instead of gold they used copper, salt, and other goods for trade. Ibn Battuta noted plenty of food and saw people well dressed in locally pro-

duced cotton clothing. He was impressed to see some houses lighted at night with candles, a luxury item in those days.

Our faithful reporter Ibn Battuta also commented that the Muslims in Mali were very devout. So strict were their teachers that they kept children chained in school each day until they had learned the required passages of the Quran!

Berber merchants and the Almoravids had already introduced Islam to Ghana before Mali rose to power. It was Mansa Musa's pilgrimage, however, that really forged strong links with the Muslim world and opened up the path for immigrants from the east. Just as in Ghana, though, Islam tended to be the religion of the wealthy aristocracy in Mali. The common folk mostly kept their ancestral beliefs. To keep everyone happy, the king had to walk a fine line between the two groups. It was a Muslim scholar who advised Musa to go to Mecca. But, to determine the best starting day for the pilgrimage, Mansa relied on an elder who used his traditional divining powers.

The Empire Falls

After Mansa Musa's death, the empire went to his son, Maghan (MAH gahn). Maghan, however, could not follow in the footsteps of the great "black Moses." He reigned for only four years, but in that short time, disaster came. Timbuktu was raided by warriors from the Volta River area. The city's mosques and schools were set afire, and its great marketplace was reduced to rubble.

Maghan's successor, Mansa Sulayman, was a capable ruler who did much to restore Mali's strength. But the fall of Timbuktu had sent a tremor through the empire. Other states saw their chance for independence. In the north, the Tuaregs took Walata and Arawan. In the west, the Tucolor and Woloff peoples seized their freedom. In the south, the Mossi attacked trading caravans and military garrisons. And in the east, the Songhay were gathering strength around their capital of Gao.

When the central power in Ghana crumbled, the kingdom broke up into its many original states and culturally defined areas. In Mali, that pattern was repeated. The empire limped on for another 200 years, but its days of glory were over.

◀ Masked dancers of a secret Dogon society perform ritual dances at a funeral ceremony. Red costumes help the dancers to drive the dead person's spirit from his house.

Songhay—From Greatness to Ruin

Sunni Ali Ber: The Warrior King

Sunni Ali Ber (soo nee AHL ee bair) was known as Ali the Great, and, indeed, he lived up to his name.

Ali Ber was a fearless warrior who ruled from the battlefield and fought alongside his soldiers. From his capital at Gao, he kept his eye on the city of Timbuktu. If he could only win that great center of Muslim learning, Ali Ber could begin to expand his small state into an empire.

Ali Ber's chance came in 1468, only four years after he had ascended the Songhay throne. The desert Tuaregs had captured Timbuktu from Mali. The Tuareg leader, Akil (ah KEEL) preferred to live in the desert and had made a man named Ammar (ahm MAHR) governor of Timbuktu.

Ammar was also the tax collector in Timbuktu. He kept one third of the money for himself and two thirds for Akil. But each time Ammar completed the tax collection, Akil swept into town with his warriors and took it all, including Ammar's share. Ammar swore revenge and hatched an evil plot. He sent a secret message to Sunni Ali Ber, his enemy, in Gao. Ammar offered to hand over the city of Timbuktu to the king if Ali Ber would drive off Akil.

Sunni Ali Ber was a shrewd leader. What did he care about this upstart Ammar! He immediately ordered his army to march on Timbuktu and personally rode at the head of the cavalry. Meanwhile, Akil and Ammar watched and waited on a hilltop near Timbuktu.

Ali Ber's soldiers advanced in ordered ranks, one after the other, in an endless flow of men and horses. The cavalry was armed with sabers and lances. Their huge brass helmets and cotton-padded breastplates gave them the appearance of giants. The foot soldiers marched with bows and poisoned arrows and had long, pointed staves at the ready.

The sight of this army sent the Tuareg chief, Akil, scurrying back into the desert. Ammar stood his ground, determined to carry out his part of the bargain. He sent a fleet of canoes across the Niger to help the army across. But as soon as the king stepped ashore, Ammar panicked and fled.

Meanwhile, the Muslim scholars at the city's university of Sankore (SAN koh ray) were also leaving as fast as they could. For years, they had scorned the Songhay as pagan infidels. They knew Ali Ber to be a Muslim only in name, one who put off his prayers for days and disregarded the ties of brotherhood that usually united Muslims. Now they feared the wrath of the Songhay king and his men. In truth, their fear was justified, for Sunni Ali Ber descended on the city like an eagle with talons extended for its prey. He slaughtered thousands of citizens. Those who had traded with the Tuaregs were tortured and dismembered, for Ali Ber considered these desert people his bitterest enemies.

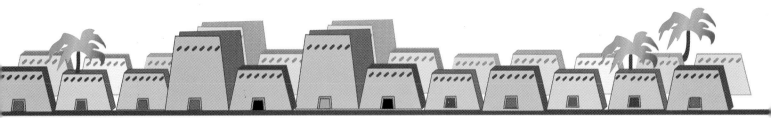

Timbuktu was now in Songhay hands. Yet there was another prize that Ali Ber coveted—the great city of Jenne (or Djenne), some 480 km (300 mi) southwest of Timbuktu. Though Jenne was not well known to the outside world, it rivaled Timbuktu as a center of commerce. Its university boasted famous medical surgeons and thousands of teachers knowledgeable in many subjects.

Ninety-nine times had Jenne withstood the attacks of the Malian kings. Ninety-nine times were the Malians defeated by the marshy swamps and intricate waterways that surrounded the city. Direct attack was impossible. Instead, Ali Ber decided to lay siege to the city. Little did he know how long the siege would last!

In the dry season, the Songhay army camped outside Jenne to prevent people and goods from entering or leaving the town. In the wet season, the river rose, surrounding the city with water. The army moved to higher ground, blockading the city with a fleet of 400 canoes. The years came and went. There was no fighting. The Songhay army cultivated its own food on the banks of the river and waited. Meanwhile, the citizens of Jenne were slowly starving to death.

Seven years, seven months, and seven days later, the city's council finally admitted defeat. The proud young king of Jenne rode into the Songhay camp to surrender. He feared for his life, but Ali Ber greeted him with respect. He admired the young man's courage and invited him to sit at his side. Thus was begun a time-honored tradition in which the kings of Jenne and the kings of Songhay shared the same royal mat.

Sunni Ali Ber then marched into Jenne. Now this jewel was his! The citizens counted their last moments, fearing that they too would be slaughtered, just like

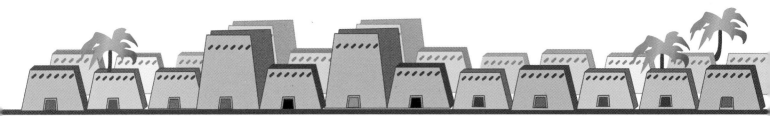

their neighbors in Timbuktu. But Ali Ber was merciful. After all, the people of Jenne had heroically survived the long years of siege, and the Songhay king loved nothing better than a courageous enemy. Indeed, so great was his desire to form a bond between Jenne and the Songhay that he married the young king's mother!

Now nothing could hold back Sunni Ali Ber. With his sights set westward, he soon gained a hold in the kingdom of Mali. To the north, he took Walata; to the east the valuable copper mines at Takedda. His raids on the neighboring Fulbe people left so few survivors that, it was said, they could all stand in the shadow of a single tree. In all directions the warrior king rode, tireless in his efforts to build an empire.

Ali Ber's enemies called him a tyrant and a bloodthirsty scoundrel. His allies praised and revered him, calling him, like a god, "the Most High." To this day, he lives on in history as Sunni Ali Ber, King Ali the Great.

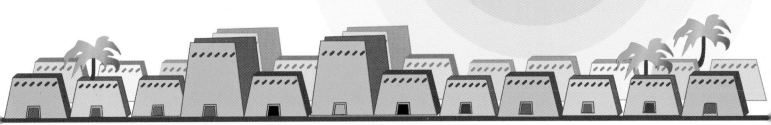

The Early Days of the Songhay

To the people who settled long ago near the middle region of the Niger, the river was known as *Isa Beri* (ee suh BE ree), "the great river." For a thousand miles, from Lake Debo around the great bend downstream to Busa, the Niger River is an easily navigable waterway. At each end of this stretch are treacherous rapids that challenge invaders coming by boat.

The Niger's banks are fertile and its waters abundant with fish. It was a good place to settle, and there are many legends that recall the origins of the Songhay people. Some say that the great ancestor, Faran Makan Bote (far RAHN mah KAHN BOH tay), was a water spirit whose

The life of the Songhay people centered on the Niger River, which dominated their environment. The river supplied water and fish, and the fertile soils on its banks could be farmed. This drawing is by Major Denham Dixon, who traveled extensively in the western Sudan in the 1820s. ▼

> "Here [at Gao] are exceeding rich merchants; and hither continually resort
> great store of Negroes which buy cloth here brought out of Barbary
> [North Africa] and Europe. Here . . . a young slave of fifteen years age is sold for
> six ducats, and so are children sold also . . . Horses bought in Europe
> for ten ducats are sold again for forty or fifty ducats apiece. A sword is here
> valued at three or four crowns and so likewise are spurs, bridles, . . . and
> spices also are sold at a high rate: but of all other commodities
> salt is most extremely dear."
> —Leo Africanus, Moorish historian, 1510

mother was a demon. Bote is said to have conquered the farming and fishing folk along the banks of the river in the region of Dendi (DEN dee) and thus founded the first Songhay settlement at Kukya (koo KEE yuh).

Another story relates that the people in this area were divided into "masters of the river" (the fishermen) and "masters of the soil" (the farmers). With the help of a magic fish, the fishermen forced the farmers to supply them with food. Sometime between the seventh and ninth centuries, the story goes, Berbers from the north or east arrived on the banks of the Niger. They scorned the magic fish and freed the farmers from the fishermen's stranglehold. In gratitude, the farmers made the leader of these Arabs their king. He was Dia Aliamen (DEE uh a LEE uh men), the first of a ruling group known as the Dia.

In 1009, the fifteenth king, Dia Kossoi (koh SOH ee), converted to Islam and decided to live in Gao. Thus, while Kukya remained the Songhay capital, Gao attracted Muslim merchants and scholars and became the most important settlement and commercial center. Like Kumbi in ancient Ghana, it was divided into two sections—one for the Muslim traders and one for the local Songhay people. Just as salt and gold had fueled trade in Ghana and Mali, so did they create prosperity for Songhay as trade routes shifted east.

The Treacherous Princes

As you may recall, Mansa Musa's forces had captured Gao in 1325, while the king was returning from his pilgrimage to Mecca, and Musa had taken two young Songhay princes hostage. They were treated not as prisoners but as respected members of the royal family at the palace in Niani. For years, these princes worked for Musa, even leading his campaigns across the empire. But, always, they plotted to return to their homeland. When Musa died in 1337, the brothers made their escape. They fled the city, with Malian guards in hot pursuit.

Once in Gao, the older brother reclaimed the throne and established the Sunni dynasty. But it was not until the fifteenth century, when the empire of Mali was greatly weakened, that Songhay could expand its holdings. Sunni Ali Ber gained a foothold in Mali, and his successors built Songhay into the largest and most powerful of all the Sudanese kingdoms.

Askia Mohammed Touré

Sunni Ali Ber died in 1492, just as Christopher Columbus was heading west to the New World. Now Ali Ber's son was king. Like his father, he professed the Muslim faith but did not practice it. The Muslims in Songhay wanted a Muslim king who would respect Islam. They planned a revolution, gathering their forces under one of Ali Ber's lieutenants named Askia Mohammed Touré (AS kee ah muh HAM med too RAY). In 1493, after a brief

battle, the young king was over-thrown, and Askia Mohammed Touré became the first of the Askia dynasty.

Mohammed Touré was a Soninke and a devout Muslim. The scholars and teachers who had fled Timbuktu returned, and the city was restored to its former status. Gao also grew, to become a prosperous city of 10,000 inhabitants or more.

Mohammed Touré saw himself as the head of all the Muslims in the western Sudan and the "renewer of the faith." He set up rigid controls to ensure that Islam was properly prac-ticed. He even had spies who

◄ The Songhay empire encompassed almost the entire western Sudan. These women of Chad may well be descendants of some of the diverse peoples embraced by the empire at its height.

prowled the streets at night and arrested any man seen talking to a woman other than his wife. Like Mansa Musa, he undertook a spectacular pilgrimage to Mecca, accompanied by thousands of slaves and soldiers. In Mecca and Medina, he gave away 100,000 pieces of gold as alms.

When Mohammed Touré returned, he set about expanding the empire through a series of holy wars, or *jihads*. He was determined to convert every nonbeliever to Islam. He took his army farther east than even the kings of Mali had ventured. He conquered the Hausa (HOU zuh) states near Lake Chad and struck the Mossi (MOH see) kingdom to the south. He secured the empire's northeastern borders against Tuareg raids. Within a few years, the Songhay empire was three times larger than Mali had been and occupied almost the entire western Sudan.

Unfortunately, Askia Mohammed Touré's last years were filled with misery. One of his own sons banished him, now almost 90 years old and blind, to an island in the Niger River. There, Mohammed Touré was tor-

mented by insects and wild animals. He was later brought back to the palace, where he died in 1538.

Government and Empire

The kingdoms of Ghana and Mali were made up of many small states that pledged allegiance to a single king. The Songhay leader Askia Mohammed Touré took the organization of power one step further.

The Songhay empire was divided into five large provinces, each with its own governor. There was a central government of ministers responsible for various departments, including the treasury, the navy (the Songhay canoe fleet), tax collection, the forests, the woodcutters, and the fishermen. Every town and village had a mayor appointed by the king. Islamic judges were appointed to every large district to do away with traditional law and administer Muslim justice. The king's court was the highest court, hearing appeals from the lower courts.

Instead of drafting men into the army when needed, Mohammed Touré created a professional fighting force. His soldiers were well trained and equipped and housed in military

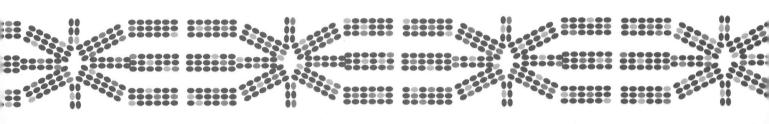

camps. They were ready to move at a moment's notice.

Askia Mohammed Touré is considered the greatest of the Songhay kings. He built the largest and wealthiest of the Sudanese kingdoms, and under his rule, Songhay became the most organized empire in precolonial Africa.

The Moroccan Invasion

The Moroccans had long profited from business with Songhay. The greedy sultan of Morocco, who was already an exceedingly wealthy man, believed that if he could control the salt and gold sources, he could become even richer. In 1585 the Sultan's forces seized the salt mines at Taghaza. Then he sent an army to attack Songhay itself.

The army was led by a Moor named Judar Pasha (JOO dahr PAH shah). He crossed the desert with some 4,000 soldiers, 600 non-combatants, and 10,000 camels. They were well trained and equipped with the best weapons that money could buy, including cannons and guns.

On the way, at least half the men died. The survivors faced a Songhay

"Judar Pasha returned to Morocco laden with treasure for the greedy sultan. He had thirty camels loaded with gold dust, a great store of valuable pepper, one hundred and twenty camel loads of special wood and horns used by the Moroccan textile and leather dyers. There were fifty horses and great numbers of slaves, as well as fifteen of the king's daughters of Gao, which were to be the Sultan's concubines."
—Jasper Tomson, Marrakesh, July 1599

army that outnumbered them by thousands. But swords, spears, and arrows were no match against the gunfire of the Moors. In 1591 first Gao and then Timbuktu fell.

This was the beginning of the end for Songhay. Because the Moors could not find the secret sources of gold, the Moroccans gave up Songhay as a lost cause. Despite spirited resistance from the Songhay army, the Moorish soldiers who occupied the Songhay cities began a reign of terror that endured well into the eighteenth century.

The historian Al Sadi, author of a book called *Tarikh es Sudan*, wrote of the times: "Security gave place to danger, wealth to poverty; distress and calamities and violence succeeded tranquility. Everywhere, men destroyed each other. In every place and in every direction there was plundering, and war spared neither life nor property nor persons."

The Songhay empire was destroyed. The Songhay people returned to the land of their ancestors, the region of Dendi, where their descendants live to this day.

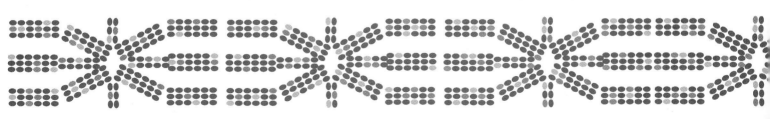

Epilogue

Several areas in Africa developed into kingdoms. Others did not. In the western Sudan, a number of kingdoms, including some not mentioned in this book, rose and fell over a period of almost a thousand years.

What happened to the western Sudan after the fall of Songhay? Why did Europe move into the industrial age and the modern era, while the western Sudan, and most of Africa, continued in its old ways?

When the Moroccans invaded Songhay, it cost them some 23,000 deaths from warfare and disease. In the long run, however, the Songhay losses were much greater, for the kingdom lost its place as the most powerful and advanced of the western Sudanese kingdoms. The government crumbled. Merchants could no longer travel the trade routes in safety, and the kingdom erupted in chaos. For the second time in the history of the Sudan (the first was when the Almoravids invaded Ghana in 1054, described in Chapter 1), a Moroccan invasion brought ruin to a vast area.

Warfare continued in the western Sudan for centuries, as one nation after another struggled for power. The area was weakened beyond repair, and no nation afterward achieved the greatness of the historic kingdoms of Ghana, Mali, and Songhay.

The western Sudan lay at the heart of a great network of nations that influenced its culture. Of these, the Moorish civilization of the North African coast was most important. It had flowered during medieval times. Its products and ideas flowed north across the Mediterranean and southward across the Sahara, linking the kingdoms of the Sudan with the markets of Europe. By the seventeenth century, though, North Africa itself had begun to decline, and the Moors no longer had the power to expand trade or to conquer new regions. The western Sudan lost its vital connection to the north.

At the same time, the Sahara became a real barrier between the Sudan and Europe. Crossing the great desert had always been a highly risky venture. Only the promise of great financial rewards had made the journey worthwhile for the Berber merchants who traveled the ancient trade routes. But with the downfall of the West African kingdoms, the merchants lost their best clients, namely the kings themselves and their royal households. Though trade across the Sahara never came to a complete halt and actually continues to this day, its volume was enormously reduced.

Meanwhile, great changes were taking place in Europe. Lured by the legendary gold of West Africa, Portuguese ships began arriving in the Gulf of Guinea in the mid-fifteenth century, just as Songhay was rising to power. On the rough Guinea shores, the Portuguese found Africans willing to trade all the gold they could dream of.

The Portuguese were soon followed by other Europeans. And once Christopher Columbus had reached the Americas in 1492, the Europeans sailing to the African coast found a commodity even more valuable than gold: the Africans themselves, who became the human cargo in the transatlantic slave trade and were destined to work in the mines and on the plantations of North and South America.

The slave trade affected mostly the African nations along the Guinea coast. But there was a ripple effect that was felt deep into the African interior, where the kingdoms of the western Sudan were struggling with their own problems.

Once Songhay had fallen (in the late sixteenth century), there was no central power to keep order in the area. Agriculture declined, and people were homeless. The vast savannah became home to thousands of refugees, fleeing both the slave raids and the warring armies of rival states. It seemed the chaos would never end.

By the late nineteenth century, the slave trade was over. But the Europeans now had an iron grip on the continent. They were in dire need of new markets for their manufactured goods. And they needed raw materials to make these goods. Africa was the solution to both problems.

In the race to claim lands and colonies for themselves, the Europeans ignored the existing ethnic ties and rivalries between the African people. By 1914 the European map of Africa was a checkerboard of French, Italian, Portuguese, German, Spanish, Belgian, and British colonies or protectorates.

The French took most of the western Sudan. In 1894, they conquered Timbuktu, and in 1898, the city of Gao. French West Africa, as the western Sudan was now called, was at last united in an uneasy colonial peace.

French administrators "encouraged" Africans to produce more raw materials, such as cotton and groundnuts, for

Bamako is the capital of modern Mali. From here, people travel by train to the Senegalese port of Dakar, or down the Niger River to Timbuktu and other river towns. Sometimes, desert nomads can be seen shopping in the city's stores. ▶

export to Europe. Regular food crops were neglected. By the 1950s the colonies had to import most of their food supplies. At the same time, relatively expensive manufactured goods were imported from Europe. More and more effort had to be put into raising cash crops for the European market so that money would be available to buy the European imports.

The French did little to develop their new territories. Roads and railways served only to transport trade goods to the sea. There was no effort to develop the interior or to build trade networks with other nations. Communications were almost nonexistent. And education was kept to the bare minimum. In addition, the French imposed a "head tax" on every adult male. They also paid peasant farmers fixed low prices for their goods, which were sold at higher prices abroad.

The French pocketed the profits as government revenue.

These were the economic problems that Mali, Niger, Chad, Burkina Faso, and Mauritania—the modern nations of former French West Africa—faced when they won independence in 1960. There were severe political problems as well. Overnight the new nations were expected to handle democracy, an idea that had taken hold in Europe only after centuries of conflict. They were expected to compete in the international trade market. To do so, they had to borrow huge sums of money from banks and other organizations to develop factories, transportation, and labor. The burden of these debts has not allowed the nations of the western Sudan to flourish. In fact, it has kept them in dire poverty. In addition, changing weather patterns

◀ Survivors of hundreds of years of political upheaval and conflict, the peoples of the western Sudan must still contend with their environment. They find that traditional ways and wisdom still serve alongside newer methods. Here, nomads draw water from a well in the age-old fashion.

seem to bring drought more often to the western Sudan than ever before.

For centuries the people of the Sudan ably met the challenge of their harsh environment. Their kingdoms were considered among the wealthiest in the known world. Their thriving market towns and great cities were internationally known centers of commerce and learning in the Middle Ages. And many of their kings went down in history as brilliant and heroic leaders.

Yet today the western Sudan is one of the poorest regions on earth. Repeated invasions, internal division, slavery, colonialism, and poor leadership, as well as years of desperate famine, have taken their toll. For now, most people in the western Sudan must depend on outside aid to survive.

Yet there is hope. Many rural people are learning how to combine their ancient knowledge of farming, fishing, and livestock with modern technology. African leaders are promoting more small-scale projects that benefit their own people, rather than the huge industrial schemes that benefited only foreign money lenders.

In time, perhaps, the western Sudan may emerge as a model for other areas currently suffering similar problems. The fabric of the Sudanese peoples' lives has not been destroyed. Hopefully it will survive into the next millennium.

Pronunciation Key

Some words in this book may be new to you or difficult to pronounce. Those words have been spelled phonetically in parentheses. The syllable that receives stress in a word is shown in small capital letters. The following pronunciation key shows how letters are used to show different sounds.

a	after	(AF tur)	oh	flow	(floh)	ch	chicken	(CHIHK un)
ah	father	(FAH thur)	oi	boy	(boi)	g	game	(gaym)
ai	care	(kair)	oo	rule	(rool)	ing	coming	(KUM ing)
aw	dog	(dawg)	or	horse	(hors)	j	job	(jahb)
ay	paper	(PAY pur)				k	came	(kaym)
			ou	cow	(kou)	ng	long	(lawng)
e	letter	(LET ur)	yoo	few	(fyoo)	s	city	(SIH tee)
ee	eat	(eet)	u	taken	(TAY kun)	sh	ship	(shihp)
				matter	(MAT ur)	th	thin	(thihn)
ih	trip	(trihp)	uh	ago	(uh goh)	thh	feather	(FETHH ur)
eye	idea	(eye DEE uh)				y	yard	(yahrd)
y	hide	(hyd)				z	size	(syz)
ye	lie	(lye)				zh	division	(duh VIHZH un)

For Further Reading

(* = Recommended for young readers)

Beckwith, Carol, and Marion Van Offelen. *Nomads of Niger*. New York: Harry N. Abrams, 1983.*

Bovill, E. W. *The Golden Trade of the Moors*. Oxford: Oxford University Press, 1968.

Boyd, Herb. *African History for Beginners*. New York: Writers and Readers Publishing, 1991.*

Brooks, Lester. *Great Civilizations of Ancient Africa*. New York: Four Winds Press, 1971.

Chu, Daniel, and Elliott Skinner. *A Glorious Age in Africa*. New York: Doubleday, Zenith Books, 1965.*

Cross, Nigel. *The Sahel: The Peoples' Right to Development*. London: SOS Sahel, 1990.

Davidson, Basil. *Africa in History*. New York: Macmillan, 1991.

Davidson, Basil. *African Kingdoms*. New York: Time-Life Books, 1966.

Davidson, Basil. *A Guide to African History*. New York: Doubleday, Zenith Books, 1965.

Davidson, Basil. *The Lost Cities of Africa*. Boston: Little, Brown, 1970.

Dobler, Lavinia G. *Great Rulers of the African Past*. New York: Doubleday, 1965.*

Fage, J.D. *The Cambridge History of Africa*. Vol. 2. Cambridge: Cambridge University Press, 1978.

Harris, Joseph E. *Africans and Their History*. New York: New American Library, 1987.

Joseph, Joan. *Black African Empires*. Franklin Watts, 1974.*

Ki-Zerbo, Joseph. *Die Geschichte Schwarz-Afrikas* [The History of Black Africa]. Wuppertal: Peter Hammer, 1979.

Kwamena-Poh, Michael. *African History in Maps*. London: Longman, 1982.

Laye, Camara. *The Guardian of the Word*. New York: Vintage Books, 1963.

Levtzion, Nehemia. *Ancient Ghana and Mali*. London: Menthuan, 1973.

McEvedy, Collin. *The Penguin Atlas of African History*. London: Penguin Books, 1980.*

Murray, Jocelyn. *Cultural Atlas of Africa*. New York: Facts on File, 1989.*

Newton, Alex. *West Africa—A Travel Survival Kit*. Australia: Lonely Planet Publications, 1992.

Oliver, Roland. *The African Experience*. New York: HarperCollins, 1991.

Oliver, Roland, and J. D. Fage. *A Short History of Africa*. 6th ed. London: Penguin Books, 1988.

Powell, A. *The Rise of Islam*. London: Warwick Press, 1980.*

Shillington, Kevin. *History of Africa*. London: Macmillan Press, 1989.

Shinnie, Margaret. *Ancient African Kingdoms*. New York: New American Library, 1965.

Stride, G. T., and C. Ifeka. *Peoples and Empires of West Africa*. New York: Africana Publishing, 1971.

Thompson, Elizabeth Bartlett. *Africa Past and Present*. Boston: Houghton Mifflin, 1966.

Index